CW00544779

THE
LITTLE
BOOK
OF
CRIME AND
PUNISHMENT

STEPHEN HALLIDAY

First published 2014

The History Press
The Mill, Brimscombe Port
Stroud, Gloucestershire, GL5 2QG
www.thehistorypress.co.uk

British Library Cataloguing in Publication Data.
A catalogue record for this book is available from the British Library.

ISBN 978 0 7509 5215 6

Typesetting and origination by The History Press
Printed in Great Britain

CONTENTS

ABOUT THE AUTHOR

Stephen Halliday was educated at Brentwood School and Pembroke College, Cambridge. After a career in industry (where he says he made his main contribution to human welfare by introducing Hellmann's Mayonnaise to Great Britain) he became a lecturer and in 1999 published his first book, *The Great Stink of London: Sir Joseph Bazalgette and the cleansing of the Victorian Metropolis*, about the great engineer who built much of Victorian London and banished cholera from the capital. He has made many television and radio programmes and regularly reviews books for newspapers and magazines. *The Little Book of Crime and Punishment* is his fifteenth book and is based on extensive research in historical archives and on his sixteen years' experience as a magistrate. He lives in Cambridge with wife Jane, a midwife at the Rosie maternity hospital, daughter Faye, a nurse, and son Simon, who works for the university.

INTRODUCTION

This short volume is the product of the author's long involvement with the criminal justice system, both as a student and participant. An earlier account of the long and often gruesome history of Newgate Prison and its neighbour the Old Bailey familiarised me with the eccentricities, injustices and brutality of the system as it existed well into the twentieth century. And sixteen years as a magistrate has taught me of the futility of the lives of many repeat offenders and the heroic patience of those who try to give them hope. In writing this book I am indebted to my friend James Wareing who, when I was falling behind with my schedule, made his tranquil home available to me in which to write without interruption. Thank you, James.

Stephen Halliday, 2014

TIMELINE OF
CRIMINAL HISTORY

1154 Henry II becomes king; Newgate starts use as a prison
1166 Grand juries first used to indict criminals
1170 Murder of Archbishop Thomas Becket following dispute
      with Henry over the benefit of clergy
1189 End of the reign of Henry II; 'Time Immemorial' in
      English Law
1198 Innocent III becomes Pope and ends involvement of clergy
      in trials by ordeal; juries take over in England
1215 Signing of Magna Carta
1361 Justices of the Peace (magistrates) first mentioned in Act of
      Parliament
1381 Peasants' Revolt, when Wat Tyler's followers destroy the
      Fleet and Newgate Prisons
1423 Richard Whittington, former mayor of London, leaves
      money to rebuild Newgate Prison
1587 Mary, Queen of Scots executed at Fotheringay
1612 Pendle witch trials
1667 Jurors released after imprisonment for refusing to find
      William Penn guilty
1685 Duke of Monmouth beheaded (incompetently) by Jack Ketch
1723 Waltham Black Act begins creation of the Bloody Code
      with its 300 capital offences
1724 Execution of serial escaper Jack Sheppard
1725 Execution of 'thief taker' Jonathan Wild
1726 Birth of John Howard, prison reformer

1728   John Gay's *The Beggar's Opera* is written, based on the career of Jonathan Wild

1741   Last use of pressing to secure a plea

1747   Novelist Henry Fielding becomes magistrate at Bow Street, later creates the Bow Street Runners

1748   Birth of Jeremy Bentham, designer of panopticon prisons

1754   Death of Henry Fielding, whose brother John takes over the Bow Street Runners and creates horse patrols

1750s   'Tyburn Drop' replaces strangulation with hanging as a method of execution

1767   Midwife Elizabeth Brownrigg executed for maltreating and killing a servant girl

1777   John Howard's report 'The state of the prisons' begins prison reform process

1780   Gordon Riots; birth of Elizabeth Fry

1783   Tyburn processions end when executions transferred to scaffold in front of Newgate

1790   Death of John Howard from 'prison fever' (typhus) contracted while visiting gaols in the Ukraine

1809   Dartmoor Prison opens

1813   Elizabeth Fry visits Newgate and begins programme of reform

1817   Elizabeth Fry secures the end of public whipping of women

1820   Cato Street Conspirators are the last criminals sentenced to be hung, drawn and quartered

1821   Millbank Panopticon Prison opens (closed 1890, now site of Tate Britain)

1822   Robert Peel becomes Home Secretary and begins to dismantle the Bloody Code

1824   John Dickens sent to Marshalsea Prison for debt; son Charles works in Warren's blacking factory

1829   Metropolitan Police founded; bodysnatcher William Burke hanged; accomplice William Hare escapes justice by turning King's evidence

1837   Pillory used for the last time

1840   Charles Dickens and William Thackeray attend execution of Francois Courvoisier outside Newgate

1868   Hangings transferred to execution chamber inside Newgate; transportation to Australia ends

1872   Stocks cease to be used as punishment

1886   First football riot, between Queen's Park Rangers fans *vs.*
        Preston North End supporters
1888   Jack the Ripper murders in Whitechapel
1902   Newgate Prison demolished to allow expansion of Old Bailey
1904   James Whitaker Wright commits suicide in the Law Courts
1916   Irish patriot Sir Roger Casement executed at Pentonville
1928   Bertold Brecht's *The Threepenny Opera* opens, based on
        John Gay's *The Beggar's Opera* two centuries earlier
1933   Last use of grand juries (formally abolished in 1948)
1937   Rev. Harold Davidson, former rector of Stiffkey, killed by a
        lion at Skegness
1944   The Great Escape: Roger Bushell leads seventy-five RAF
        personnel out of Stalag Luft III; Helen Duncan is the last
        person to be imprisoned under the Witchcraft Act of 1735
1953   Derek Bentley hanged for murder actually carried out by
        accomplice Christopher Craig
1955   Ruth Ellis becomes the last woman to be executed in Britain
1962   Petty criminal James Hanratty executed for A6 murder and
        'Pardon Hanratty' campaign begins
1963   Great Train Robberyw
1964   Last executions in Britain; Peter Allen and Gwynne Evans
        hanged for murder in course of robbery
1965   Great Train Robber Ronnie Biggs escapes from Wandsworth
        Gaol; Roger Casement's body transferred to Dublin
1966   Spy George Blake escapes from Wormwood Scrubs and
        makes his way to Moscow
1972   Beheading removed from the statute book
1974   *Porridge* character Norman Stanley Fletcher (portrayed by
        Ronnie Barker) enters Slade Prison
1998   Treason and piracy removed from statute book as
        capital crimes
2001   Ronnie Biggs returns voluntarily from Brazil and is gaoled
2002   DNA tests support James Hanratty's guilt; Elizabeth Fry
        featured on £5 note
2013   Death of Bruce Reynolds, mastermind of the Great Train
        Robbery; train robber Gordon Goody announces that he
        will reveal the identity of 'The Ulsterman', the insider on
        the robbery who escaped justice
2013   Death of Ronnie Biggs

1

WHY WASTE MONEY ON PRISONS?

PUT 'EM IN THE CLINK

Before the nineteenth century, criminals were rarely sentenced to prison. Prisons were expensive to build, no one was keen on having one in their backyard and it seemed a pity to waste money on criminals. The purpose of a prison (often known as the bridewell, clink or lockup to give a few local expressions) was to hold prisoners until their trials before magistrates or a judge and jury. When the trial had been held (and the usual verdict was 'guilty'), the convicted prisoner would be sent back to prison for a brief period before the sentence was carried out.

THE KING'S JUDGES

The system started with King Henry II (1154–89) who, when not quarrelling with Thomas Becket, was reforming the English legal system. And as we will see later, Henry had a strong case in his argument with the troublesome priest, even if he did overplay his hand by turning his archbishop into a martyr. Henry instituted the system whereby the king's judges, sometimes referred to as justices in eyre, travelled from Westminster to each county in his kingdom to administer justice. They normally travelled in pairs and before they arrived in a town, the local ne'er-do-wells would be rounded up by the parish constable and incarcerated in the local gaol to await trial by the king's judges. The 'judges' were unlikely to have had much in the way of legal training; the Inns of Court, where barristers and judges were later trained, did not appear for another two centuries. Henry's judges were more likely to be courtiers and nobles who enjoyed the king's confidence and were prepared to do the work at little cost.

The trials became known as assizes, derived from an old French word meaning a legal process carried out while seated. The assizes would begin with the arrival of judges, who would often process through the town with the mayor and other dignitaries before beginning the trials. This continued until 1972, when the assizes were replaced by permanently staffed Crown Courts, of which the Old Bailey is the most famous. When they had finished their work in a county, the judges would return to London and to Westminster Hall where the high court was based, until the reign of Queen Victoria who opened the present Royal Courts of Justice in the Strand in 1882. The judges would compare notes with their colleagues who had been administering justice in other parts of the kingdom, discussing such matters as how evidence was gathered and presented, what credence was attached to testimony from people at different levels in society and what penalties they had imposed for various offences.

In this way a set of common principles or precedents developed to ensure a degree of consistency in the administration of justice. In time this became known as the common law, the application of which is based upon precedents in order to combine consistency with justice. Henry II is thus regarded as the 'Father of the Common Law' and it is not by chance that the year of his death, 1189, is regarded as time immemorial in English law. If an individual can prove, for example, that he has owned a piece of land or other possession since 1189 then no claim prior to that date will be held valid in English law. The Crown Courts continue to hear serious cases which are likely, in the event of guilt being established, to result in long prison sentences.

LOCAL JUSTICE

Less serious infringements of the law would be dealt with not at the assizes by the king's judges, but by quarter sessions or petty sessions. Quarter sessions were held, as their name implies, four times a year at Epiphany (early January), Easter (March/April), Midsummer and Michaelmas (late September). They would be presided over by three Justices of the Peace sitting with a jury. Minor offences such as drunkenness, theft of fairly low-value items and most motoring offences would be dealt with by three Justices of the Peace without a jury, in petty sessions which were often held in a church hall or pub rather than in a purpose-built courthouse. The office of Justices of the Peace (also called magistrates) is an ancient one. It was first mentioned in an Act of Parliament in 1361 but the reference there is clearly to an office that had already existed for some time. In 1195, during the reign of Richard I (1189–99), Keepers of the Peace were appointed and they were probably the forerunners of the Justices of the Peace. They were chosen by the king's local representative, the sheriff, as citizens of good standing with local knowledge and they did much more than hear cases. Their knowledge of the local populace would be used to round up suspects before the assizes or quarter sessions were held (whereas nowadays a justice who knows anything about the criminal past of a suspect is required to stand down from hearing the case). They were not paid (they still aren't) and now have some training in court procedure, but they are assisted by a legally qualified court clerk who advises them, when required, on the law. Before the reign of Queen Victoria they did much else besides. In effect they were the local government authority outside the major towns, with the task of raising money from rates to repair bridges and roads, for example.

BETTER THAN DROWNING

The use of judges, magistrates and juries was a great improvement on what went before. In the early medieval period, trial by ordeal was a common method of establishing guilt or innocence, based upon the assumption that God would care for the innocent. The most common variations were trial by fire and trial by water.

Trial by fire involved walking across hot coals or holding a red-hot piece of metal. After an interval of about three days, the resulting wounds would be examined by a priest, who would decide whether the healing process had advanced sufficiently to show that the deity had indeed intervened. If not, the suspect would be declared guilty.

Trial by water took two forms. The first required the suspect to remove a stone from the bottom of a cauldron of boiling water, following which a priest would decide whether the injuries were consistent with guilt or innocence. The other form, known as ordeal by cold water, involved the accused being thrown into a river or pond, sometimes bound hand and foot. If he floated he was innocent and if he sank he would drown – regarded as a satisfactory outcome to those who believed this was a punishment for his guilt.

In 1215 Pope Innocent III (1198–1215) prohibited priests from participating in these 'ordeals', which put an end to the practice, though in the seventeenth century in England a witch-hunter called Matthew Hopkins briefly revived a form of ordeal by water associated with catching witches. It was assumed that a witch, having renounced her baptism, would be rejected by water. The unfortunate woman would be thrown into water. If she floated, she was rejected by the water and therefore guilty. If she sank, well, that was hard luck but at least she was innocent. In the absence of these crude, swift and unjust methods of determining guilt, other methods had to be found and in England this was the jury.

'GOOD MEN AND TRUE'

The first type of jury was the grand jury, which was created in England by Henry II in 1166. The word 'jury' is derived from a Norman French word meaning 'to swear' and simply meant that a number of local citizens would swear to deliver justice. The grand jury would consider evidence of a crime presented by a prosecutor and decide whether the case was strong enough to proceed to an indictment (in effect an accusation) before the assizes or quarter sessions. This was not a trial. The grand jury only considered the prosecution's case to decide whether there was sufficient evidence to proceed to a trial.

In England, grand juries ceased to operate in 1933, though they were not officially abolished until 1948. The number of jurymen on a grand jury varied, but it was never fewer than twelve and often more. They continue to be used in some parts of the world which practise the common law, notably the United States of America. Their work in England is now done by magistrates who decide whether there is a *prima facie* case to go to trial, either in the magistrates' court itself or, for more serious indictable offences, in the Crown Court. All criminal matters, from speeding to murder, begin their journey in magistrates' courts and 95 per cent of them are disposed of there. The remaining 5 per cent go to the Crown Court to be heard before a judge and a jury which is, strictly, a petit or petty jury (small jury) consisting of twelve 'good men and true'; this phrase originates in the seventeenth century to describe the trial jury though in the twentieth century women also began to serve on juries. The jury system was implicitly recognised in 1215 in Magna Carta, the same year that Pope Innocent III effectively ended trial by ordeal. The famous clause 39 of the document sealed by a reluctant King John at Runnymede in 1215 states:

> No freeman shall be taken or imprisoned or disseised [i.e dispossessed] or exiled or in any way destroyed, nor will we go upon him nor send upon him, except by the lawful judgment of his peers or by the law of the land.

The word 'peers' means that citizens have the right to be tried by their fellow citizens. Clause 40 adds that 'To no one will we sell, to no one will we refuse or delay, right or justice.' These clauses, which remain a feature of the English legal system, were taken in later centuries to mean that jury trial (i.e judgement by one's fellow citizens) was the right of any subject for serious criminal charges.

WHAT TO DO WITH THE CONVICTS

So in the absence of prison sentences, what was to happen to those who were convicted? As previously noted, not many offenders were sent to prison. In 1582 William Lambarde, a barrister of Lincoln's Inn, applauded the English penal code for no longer including 'pulling out the tongue for false rumours, cutting off the nose for adultery or taking away the privy parts for counterfeiting of money', though many equally gruesome punishments remained, which Lambarde divided into three categories: infamous, pecuniary and corporal. Infamous punishments were reserved for crimes such as treason, and pecuniary penalties were usually imposed by Justices of the Peace. Corporal punishments he divided into two subcategories: 'Capital (or deadly) punishment is done sundry ways as by hanging, burning, boiling or pressing. Not capital is of diverse forms as of cutting off the hand or ear, burning, whipping, imprisoning, stocking, setting in the pillory or ducking stool'. Imprisonment is there, but low down in the list of penalties. Some of the more common sentences were:

Fines were commonly imposed for petty offences including swearing, playing a prohibited musical instrument, sport on the Sabbath or failing to attend church. Some sports, such as football, were forbidden at any time because, in the words of an edict of 1314, of 'great noise in the city caused by hustling over large balls from which many evils may arise'.

Fines were also applied to tradesmen who sold defective produce. An alternative punishment in such cases was humiliation. For example, a fishmonger or butcher who had sold produce of poor quality or a baker whose loaves were underweight would be paraded around the town in a cart with the offending merchandise, with a placard describing his offence hanging around his neck.

The stocks, in which culprits were held by their ankles, were sometimes used to detain offenders in the hours before their appearances in court. In 1384 two defendants failed to appear for their trials because they had been put in the stocks and forgotten. Their feet froze and they died.

The City of London's stocks were in the heart of the Square Mile and in about 1282 the City's stocks market, a market for fruit and vegetables, was established nearby. It continued to trade until it made way for the residence of the Lord Mayor, the Mansion House, in 1737. Some historians believe that the stockmarket, which began to trade in stocks and shares from nearby coffee houses in the early eighteenth century, took its name from this market and hence from the stocks from which the fruit and vegetable market took its name.

In some cases the stocks were used as a punishment in their own right, usually for petty thieves, drunks and vagabonds. They remained in use in England until 1872. Passers-by were invited – some would say encouraged – to throw things at them, but at least the victims could defend themselves by catching some of the missiles.

Helpless in the pillory.

The pillory was similar to the stocks but the victims were instead held by the wrists and neck, leaving them without any protection at all. Some people died in the pillory from being struck by hard objects like stones, such as the perjurer John Waller, who was pelted to death in London in 1732. Waller was a highwayman, condemned for providing false evidence which led to the execution of a man called James Dalton. Dalton's brother delivered the coup de grâce that ended Waller's life in the pillory.

Another unfortunate was a man called Penedo who was pilloried in 1570 for forging the seal of the Court of Queen's Bench. His ears were nailed to the pillory and when he was released he left part of them behind.

Daniel Defoe had an easier time in the pillory. The author of *Robinson Crusoe* was committed to the pillory in London in 1703 for a pamphlet called 'The Shortest Way with Dissenters', which lampooned the government. Such was Defoe's popularity that he was protected from assailants by a London mob who threw flowers. Upon his release Defoe escaped the punitive fine which had also been imposed

A victim of the pillory meets his fate.

as part of his sentence by making an ignoble deal with the leader of the Tory government, Robert Harley, to become a government agent and provide intelligence about his former Whig friends.

The most unlikely candidate for the pillory was the Scottish naval officer Thomas Cochrane (1775–1860), who was feared by the forces of Napoleon as much as Nelson was. Cochrane was convicted of spreading false rumours about the death of Napoleon in order to gain from the rise in the value of shares. The evidence was strong, the verdict 'guilty' but the sentence, to stand in the pillory, was revoked for fear of provoking a riot in support of the naval hero. Instead he was fined and stripped of his knighthood, though the title was later restored by a sympathetic Queen Victoria.

The last person to be pilloried in England was Peter James Bossy, who was convicted of perjury in 1830. He was offered the choice of seven years' transportation or an hour in the pillory, and chose the pillory. He survived but disappeared from history, the punishment itself being formally abolished on 30 June 1837.

The ducking stool was a punishment used exclusively for women, commonly for prostitutes and scolds. A scold was defined as

A scold awaits a ducking.

'a troublesome and angry woman who by brawling and wrangling amongst her neighbours breaks the public peace, increases discord and becomes a public nuisance to the neighbourhood'. Nowadays we have ASBOs (antisocial behaviour orders) instead. It was also used, long after Innocent III banned the participation of clergy in trial by water, to establish whether a woman was a witch.

The ducking stool – punishment for scolds and witches.

Another way to silence a scold: the scold's bridle.

Whipping was a common punishment for vagabonds and others who disturbed the king's peace. Sometimes the culprit was restrained in the pillory, but specially designed whipping posts were also used, both in public places and within prisons where they were used to maintain discipline. The prison reformer Elizabeth Fry (1780–1845) successfully campaigned to end the public whipping of women in 1817 but the practice continued within prisons in Britain until 1948. Sometimes particularly notorious offenders would be 'whipped at the cart's tail', so tied to a cart and drawn around a town or city as they were whipped.

One of the best known (and perhaps most deserving) victims of this punishment was the perjurer Titus Oates (1649–1705). An early career as an Anglican priest was ended by accusations of blasphemy and buggery, whereupon he briefly entered the Jesuit order in France. He took advantage of anxieties about Catholic traitors in the reign of Charles II by falsely accusing a number of prominent citizens of plotting to assassinate Charles II and replace him with the king's Catholic brother (who eventually assumed the throne as James II). Many innocent people suffered gruesome deaths as traitors on the strength of Oates's perjured evidence. In 1685 he was finally convicted of perjury and sentenced to be whipped from Newgate to Tyburn and pilloried every year. It was assumed that this would result in his death but despite the fact that, according to a contemporary account, Oates 'made hideous bellowings and swooned several times with the greatness of the anguish', he survived and was released from Newgate in 1688, dying in 1705 still admired by some Protestants.

Justices of the Peace would sometimes order the whipping of vagabonds beyond the parish boundary so that they were no charge upon the parish in which they were detained. In 1572 an Act for the Punishment of Vagabonds prescribed that 'fortune tellers, pedlars, players [i.e actors]

A birch at the ready.

and jugglers' should be whipped and 'burned through the right ear' as evidence of their offence, but fortunately for William Shakespeare, who was 8 years old when the Act was passed, players who were patronised by the monarch or prominent nobles were exempt from the penalty. In 1744 an Act specified that while 'idle and disorderly persons, rogues and vagabonds' were to be publicly whipped, 'incorrigible rogues' (repeat offenders) were to be offered to the army or navy, many of them no doubt serving in the forces of Nelson and Wellington, the latter describing his troops as 'the scum of the earth'.

Mutilation was adjusted according to the crime and included: branding, cutting off of hands, feet, noses, ears and removal of eyes, tongues and lips. Counterfeiting was treated with particular savagery, with coiners, as they were called, having their right hands lopped off (presumably because they had done the counterfeiting), followed by castration.

Poaching the king's deer was also treated severely: a first offence by a serf leading to the loss of his right hand and a second offence bringing death. In the Anglo-Saxon period, the Danes would remove eyes, scalps and flay living victims.

Transportation was used as a punishment from the late sixteenth century, first to the North American colonies, though this ceased after the War of Independence, when the new USA declined to accept any more British criminals. Thereafter convicts were sent first to South Africa and later, more notoriously, to Australia, a practice which continued until the 1860s, by which date about 160,000 convicts had been resettled there. The convicts were sent from prisons like Newgate to prison ships (hulks) moored in the Thames and the Medway to await the long journey halfway round the world.

Some feared transportation more than they feared death. In June 1789 the *Morning Chronicle* reported that Mrs Maria Fitzherbert (illegally married to the Prince of Wales, later George IV) had attended the Old Bailey to hear a 16-year-old maid, Sarah Cowan, resisting attempts to persuade her to accept transportation rather than execution. She eventually succumbed and was duly sent to a life in the new colony.

Convicts being taken from Newgate to the hulks for transportation to America. American Independence later redirected them to Australia, a process which continued until the 1860s. (*The Newgate Calendar*).

THE ULTIMATE PENALTY

The ultimate penalty, of course, was death and by the end of the eighteenth century almost 300 offences were subject to capital punishment, ranging from theft of goods worth 5s (25p) and impersonating a Chelsea pensioner to arson, murder and treason. In practice the harsh penalties were often evaded, either because juries refused to convict people of petty theft or because the death sentences were set aside by the crown. But when the sentence was carried out there were many ways of taking a life.

Beheading was the kindest form of execution, if carried out by a proficient executioner, because it was instant. For this reason it was mostly reserved for royalty or the nobility, like Anne Boleyn or Thomas More. However, if the axeman was incompetent or drunk then it was a gruesome experience. Thomas Cromwell's execution in 1540 was botched, in the words of a contemporary, by 'a ragged butcherly miser which very ungoodly performed the Office' with several blows of the axe being needed to despatch the unfortunate fallen favourite of Henry VIII. The executioner was probably drunk as a result of libations supplied to him by Cromwell's aristocratic enemies, who resented their earlier humiliations at the hands of the upstart Cromwell and wanted his end to be as degrading and painful as possible.

Hanging was the usual fate of more common criminals. It was usually carried out in public until 1868, the best known execution site being Tyburn (Marble Arch). From 1868, executions were carried out within prisons before a few official witnesses. Prior to about 1850 most of those hanged died from strangulation, which could take as long as 20 minutes.

Thereafter, the longer 'Tyburn drop' brought about the breaking of the neck and instant death. James Boswell, biographer of Samuel Johnson, witnessed an execution at Tyburn before the introduction of the drop method and was so distressed by what he saw that he was unable to sleep. He advocated a more 'humane' way that he had witnessed in Rome, where 'the criminal is placed upon a scaffold and the executioner knocks him on the head with a great iron hammer then cuts his throat with a large knife and lastly hews him into pieces. The spectators are struck with prodigious terror; yet the poor wretch who is stunned into insensibility by the blow does not actually suffer much.'

Crowds gather at Tyburn (Marble Arch) to witness executions.

Burning at the stake was the fate of heretics and women who were convicted of murdering their husbands or of counterfeiting money (male forgers being hung, drawn and quartered) and occasionally of witches, though these were more often hanged. Joan of Arc suffered the fate of a heretic, having been convicted of heresy on very doubtful grounds, as did many Catholic and Protestant martyrs at Smithfield, victims of the notoriously fickle religious affiliations of Tudor monarchs.

Merciful executioners would try to ensure that victims were suffocated by smoke inhalation or strangled before the flames reached them, but some victims showed remarkable resilience. Thomas Cranmer, executed in 1556 under Queen Mary I for his Protestant faith, is said to have held his 'unworthy hand' in the flames at the stake in Oxford because it had been the hand by which he had earlier written a recantation of his Protestant beliefs, a recantation which he regretted.

In 1726 Catherine Hayes was burned for killing her husband. The executioner's attempts to strangle her beforehand were frustrated when the flames, already kindled, reached him before he had completed the task. He leapt from the blaze and left the unfortunate woman to her fate while 'the spectators beheld her pushing away the faggots while she rent the air with her cries and lamentations'.

The last person to be burned at the stake in England was Catherine Murphy, who suffered the fate at Newgate on 18 March 1789. Along with her husband and other men, she had been found guilty of treason for 'clipping' coins (shaving off some metal to make more coins). The penalty for men was hanging and for women burning, though on this occasion the executioner ensured that she was dead from hanging before burning her corpse. The Treason Act of the following year prescribed hanging for women as well as for men.

Boiling was an infamous punishment reserved for those who murdered, or attempted to murder, a master, an offence known as petty treason. In 1531 this was the fate of a man called Richard Rouse (or Roose), cook to the Bishop of Rochester, who had attempted to murder the bishop with poison and inadvertently killed several colleagues.

Catherine Hayes 'rent the air with her cries'.

Hung, drawn and quartered was an infamous punishment Edward I inflicted on rebels, notably upon the Scottish hero William Wallace in 1305 at Smithfield, where there is a plaque recording the fact set into the wall of St Bartholomew's Hospital. The victim would be dragged on a hurdle from prison to the place of execution, usually before jeering crowds and hung until almost, but not quite, dead. He would then be cut down, castrated and disembowelled and finally cut into several pieces, the head being impaled upon a stake and exhibited in a prominent place (such as London Bridge) while the other body parts would be despatched to other parts of the kingdom as a warning to others.

The Gunpowder Plot conspirators were condemned to this fate in 1606, but Guy Fawkes managed to evade the more gruesome aspects of the punishment by jumping from a ladder and breaking his neck. The last to be condemned to this form of execution were the Cato Street conspirators who, in 1820, had plotted to murder the entire Cabinet and seize power. The plot was thoroughly infiltrated

The executioner at his grim task: disembowelling a victim. (Library of Congress, LC-USZ62-119891)

and the conspirators seized in their Cato Street, Marylebone hideaway. The executioner ensured that all the condemned were dead from strangulation before cutting down their bodies and removing the heads. As was customary, he raised each head in turn and called out, 'Behold the head of a traitor,' unfortunately dropping one of them which provoked the cry of 'butterfingers' from the watching crowd.

The head of Oliver Cromwell met a different fate. Upon his death in 1658, the Lord Protector received a state funeral and was buried in Westminster Abbey. After the restoration of Charles II, Cromwell's body was disinterred, 'executed' at Tyburn and his head impaled on a stake above Westminster Hall. One wet evening it fell off and was picked up by a soldier who took it home and hid it in his chimney. It then passed through various hands, including those of a Swiss collector of 'curiosities', a drunken actor called Russell who may have been related to Cromwell by marriage, a London museum owner and a family called Wilkinson, who arranged for a full forensic examination of the head by experts who concluded in 1930 that there was 'moral certainty' that the head was indeed that of Cromwell. In 1960 the head was buried in the antechapel of Sidney Sussex College, Cambridge, which Cromwell had attended as an undergraduate. Its precise location is known to only a select few.

Pressing to death or *peine forte et dure* was a form of execution by default. If a prisoner pleaded not guilty but was found guilty, his possessions would pass to the state, leaving his family destitute. If he refused to enter a plea then his family retained his possessions but, in the words of Sir Thomas Smith written in 1583, 'he is judged mute, that is dumb by contumacy, and his condemnation is to be pressed to death, which is one of the cruellest deaths that may be.' One of the most celebrated victims of this process was a Major Strangways who, in 1659, was accused of killing his brother-in-law. Wishing to preserve his estate for his heirs, he refused to enter a plea whereupon Lord Chief Justice Glynn pronounced:

> That he be put into a mean house, stopped from any light, and be laid upon his back, with his body bare; that his arms be stretched forth with a cord, the one to one side, the other to the other side of the prison, and in like manner his legs be used; and that upon his body be laid as much iron and stone as he can bear, and more. The first day he shall have three morsel of barley bread, and the next he shall drink thrice of the water in the next channel to the prison door, but of no spring or fountain water, and this shall be his punishment till he die.

Pressing to death a man who refuses to enter a plea.

An alternative means of securing a plea, usually applied to women, was to screw the thumb with whipcord. At the Old Bailey in 1721 this was applied to Mary Andrews. The first three cords broke but she succumbed with the fourth.

Few could endure such suffering, though Strangways died under the torture, thereby preserving his estate for his heirs. The penalty lasted until 1741, when it was last used at the Cambridge Assizes.

Given the variety of penalties available to judges and magistrates, it is not surprising that few sentences of imprisonment were imposed. In the 1790s Newgate, London's most notorious prison, contained only five prisoners actually serving sentences, with many more awaiting trial or other forms of punishment. One of the five was Lord George Gordon, who had set fire to the prison in the Gordon Riots of 1780, and another was Rhynwick Williams, an artificial flower maker who had been (almost certainly wrongly) convicted of being the Newgate Monster – his story is told in Chapter 12. In the nineteenth century, however, the idea of prisons as places where criminals could be reformed took hold and a prison-building programme ensued, changing the face of the British criminal justice system. Many of the prisons are still in use.

GET OUT OF JAIL FREE

If all else failed, a fugitive from justice could always seek sanctuary a stone's throw from Newgate Prison. In 1056, in the reign of Edward the Confessor, two of the king's cousins founded the College of St Martin-le-Grand. From 1439 it offered sanctuary to thieves and debtors, though Jews and traitors were turned away. Well-informed criminals continued to take advantage of this opportunity to escape the axe, the noose or worse until the arrangement came to an end in 1697.

2

AS BLACK AS NEWGATE'S KNOCKER

CLAIMS TO INFAMY

Many prisons have left their mark on history. In London, Wormwood Scrubs, Wandsworth and Pentonville have often been in the news, sometimes with embarrassment when infamous criminals like Ronnie Biggs escaped from Wandsworth or the traitor George Blake from Wormwood Scrubs. Oscar Wilde spent time in Pentonville, where Dr Crippen, Neville Heath and the innocent Timothy Evans were all hanged. In the United States, Sing Sing Prison in New York and Alcatraz in San Fransisco Bay have their own places in history. But surely none can challenge London's Newgate Prison for longevity or notoriety. There have in fact been five Newgate Prisons and they gave the language the phrase 'as black as Newgate's knocker'. This saying dates from at least the eighteenth century and refers to the dark deeds perpetrated in the prison, as well as to the knocker on its front door being black and large.

OLDER THAN WE THOUGHT

In his *A Survey of London*, first published in 1598, the Tudor chronicler John Stow informed his readers that, unlike London's

Roman Gates (Aldgate, Bishopsgate, Aldersgate, Cripplegate, Ludgate, the Postern gate near the Tower of London and Bridgegate, opening onto London Bridge), Newgate was of medieval date and built during the reign of Henry I (1100–35). It was not until the last Newgate Prison was demolished in 1902 to make way for the extension of its partner in crime, the Old Bailey courthouse, that Stow was shown to be in error. Following the demolition, the site was excavated in preparation for the new courts and archaeologists were called to view what were clearly remains of an ancient structure. Upon examination these proved to be unmistakeably Roman, suggesting that Newgate, as it was mistakenly called in later centuries, was as old as the other Roman gates. The prefix 'New' probably refers to a rebuilding or refurbishment of the gatehouse which occurred in Anglo-Saxon times.

'THE SAFEKEEPING OF HIS PRISONERS'

Roman and medieval gatehouses were, in effect, small castles whose function was to close the gate in the city wall at night to exclude potential enemies. They would be fortified like the entrance to a castle and, of course, secure, which made them well suited to acting as lockups. As indicated, imprisonment at this time was rarely used as a sentence since it was expensive, with more imaginative and often more gruesome means being used to punish offenders. Prisons, including gatehouses, were used to hold prisoners for short periods before their trials (in Newgate's case at the adjacent courthouse, the Old Bailey) or for an equally short period prior to the infliction of punishment such as whipping, branding or execution.

The gatehouse was probably used as a lock-up from the reign of Henry II (1154–89) but by the reign of Henry III (1216–70), despite being patched up and rebuilt by the Anglo-Saxons, it was in a sufficiently decrepit state for the young king to order that the Sheriffs of the City 'repair the gaol of Newgate for the safe keeping of prisoners' in 1218.

In 1241 Henry, short of money, threatened to lock up London's Jews in Newgate unless they paid him 20,000 marks and in 1253 he gaoled the city sheriffs for a time because they had allowed a prisoner to escape from Newgate who had allegedly killed the queen's cousin.

The gaol was also used as one of a number of sites which exhibited the heads of prisoners who had been executed.

'EASE AND LICENCE' AND DEATH FROM TYPHUS

By 1400 the condition of Newgate was beginning to cause concern to the mayor, aldermen and Sheriffs of the City who were responsible for it. Thomas Knowles, a grocer, paid for a supply of fresh water to the gaol from St Bartholomew's Hospital and, in the interests of decorum, a tower was built adjacent to the gaol to house female prisoners. The old Ludgate gatehouse nearby was opened to accommodate debtors and fraudsters (as distinct from the common criminals held in Newgate), but some of them found Ludgate so comfortable that they were happy to remain there. An indignant mayor declared that many of them were 'willing to take up their abode there so as to waste and spend their goods upon the ease and licence that there is within'. The complacent inmates were duly despatched to Newgate, where sixty of them died from 'gaol fever' (typhus).

A LEGENDARY ORPHAN AND HIS CAT

A new mayor, Richard Whittington (he was never Sir Richard) was a man of more humane disposition. Much of the pantomime legend is true. He was born in 1359 and came from the hamlet of Pauntley, in Gloucestershire. He was the younger son of Sir William Whittington, a Member of Parliament and local landowner, who died at about the time Richard was born (hence the 'orphan' legend) and Richard later married Alice Fitzwaryn, the daughter of another Gloucestershire landowner.

Like many younger sons of gentry, Richard was sent to London to earn his living and became a member of the Mercers' company, London's grandest livery company, whose members dealt in woollen cloth, the most important commodity in England's overseas trade and the foundation of London's increasing wealth. He enjoyed the confidence of successive monarchs and in 1415 he was nominated by King Henry V as one of only four prominent citizens whose permission had to be sought before any building could be demolished. He was also put in charge of the rebuilding of Westminster Abbey.

He was buried in the medieval church of St Michael Paternoster where in 1949, during excavations in the vicinity of Whittington's tomb, builders found the mummified remains of a cat.

In 1419 Richard had become Lord Mayor for the fourth time and one of his first acts was to address the state of Newgate Prison and the deaths that were occurring there. In November of that year he issued a proclamation that declared, 'By reason of the foetid and corrupt atmosphere that is in the heinous gaol of Newgate many persons are now dead who would be alive'. He reopened Ludgate to reduce the overcrowding in Newgate and on his death, in 1423, he left money to 're-edify [i.e rebuild] the gaol of Newgate'. There is no pictorial record of this gaol, which survived for over two centuries until the Great Fire of London in 1666 destroyed it as the fire reached its north-western extremity. In honour of its builder it was known as The Whit, and the gaol which replaced it after the fire bore the same nickname.

THE NEW WHIT

The New Whit was completed in 1672 and occupied a small site, measuring only about 26m by 16m, though it was five storeys in height and closely resembled a medieval gatehouse, as its predecessor presumably did. It often featured in engravings during the eighteenth century, from which is it possible to see that the building had a number of niches, each occupied by a statue (the number of niches varying according to the whims of the artist). Three niches were recorded as containing statues representing peace, security and plenty. The antiquarian Thomas Pennant (1726–98) compiled a catalogue of the City's prominent buildings in the eighteenth century and was writing shortly before the New Whit, the third Newgate, was demolished in the 1780s. He wrote that a fourth niche contained Whittington's statue 'with the cat, which remained in a niche to its final demolition, on the rebuilding of the present prison'. A sixteenth-century portrait of Whittington, now lost, also featured a cat. Cats were often associated with good fortune, which may explain the connection with the prosperous city merchant and its later entry into pantomime legend.

A GAOL WITH A WINDMILL

Conditions in the New Whit were not much better than they had been in Whittington's time. Gaol fever was often rife, the infection carried from one prisoner to another by lice which were carried by rats and so often associated with filthy, overcrowded conditions. The authorities remained complacent about the deaths of prisoners but they became alarmed when, in 1750, forty-three officials died of typhus, including a judge in the Old Bailey, the Lord Mayor and a number of jurymen. It was believed, with some reason, that foul air and poor ventilation created conditions in which typhus could thrive, so they installed a windmill on the roof of the prison which was designed to improve the circulation of air.

The windmill was designed by Dr Stephen Hales (1677–1761), a clergyman scientist who advocated the distillation of drinking water from seawater and improved ventilation in all buildings where people gathered. He was thinking along the right lines, but unfortunately seven of the eleven labourers employed to install the windmill died of typhus, which they contracted while carrying out the work. The windmill is a prominent feature of eighteenth-century prints of the prison during its last decades, but it did little to improve the appalling conditions in the prison and the City authorities decided to replace the old gatehouse-style prison with a more modern design.

A VERY SHORT LIFE: 'CONDUCTED THROUGH THE STREETS IN THEIR CHAINS'

The fourth Newgate, construction of which began in 1770, was a much larger building, occupying a site 500m long, with far more accommodation for prisoners, though still lying adjacent to the Old Bailey. It was built at a time when penal reformers were starting to believe that prisons could be used for sentences rather than as temporary holding places. It was designed by George Dance the Younger (1741–1825), the City of London architect.

Dance's first Newgate had the shortest life of all Newgates. It was completed in 1778, but in 1780 it was attacked by the Gordon Rioters led by a deranged aristocrat called Lord George Gordon (1751–93). Gordon, enraged by some moderate measures to reduce the penalties imposed on Roman Catholics by Tudor and Stuart laws, led a mob variously estimated as between 20,000 and 60,000 rioters in attacks upon Catholic chapels, sympathisers and, for reasons that were not clear, Newgate gaol. In reference to the medieval practice whereby judges 'delivered' prisoners from prison to trial, one artist of the time described his depiction of the burning prison as 'a new species of gaol delivery'.

The mayhem was witnessed by a number of prominent citizens, including the artist William Blake and Dr Johnson's biographer, James Boswell, who described the looters at the prison as they 'did their work at leisure, in full security, without sentinels, without trepidation, as men lawfully employed, in full day.' One witness described the process by which the mob gained access to the gaol via its few windows. A young man, standing upon the shoulders of another, broke the first-floor windows by banging his head against them. He climbed through the shattered glass, followed by others who joined him in making a bonfire of furniture and other moveable objects, which created a conflagration that reduced the prison to a smouldering ruin. Three hundred prisoners had already been released and, in the words of the writer George Crabbe, 'They were conducted through the streets in their chains. You have no conception of the frenzy of the multitude'.

Charles Dickens later made the Gordon Riots the subject of his novel *Barnaby Rudge*. Many were hanged following the riots, though not Lord George Gordon, who claimed that he intended to make a peaceful protest.

THE FIFTH AND FINAL NEWGATE

The prison was immediately rebuilt and reopened in 1783, one of its earliest inmates being none other than Lord George Gordon who, having escaped the scaffold for his part in the riots, was gaoled for making insulting comments about Marie Antoinette, Queen of France, who was yet to meet her own end. While in Newgate the renegade lord converted to Judaism and shortly afterwards died, perhaps of gaol fever. The new building was deliberately grim and forbidding and a later City architect wrote that 'with its narrow windows and gloomy yards it seems to me to have been about as hopelessly human as it is possible to imagine.'

ENTER THE NEWGATE DROP: 'A HIDEOUS AND DEGRADING SIGHT'

The opening of the final Newgate coincided with a decision to cease the practice of executing the condemned at Tyburn, on the present site of Marble Arch. These gruesome occasions are described in a later chapter, but from 1783 hangings were carried out on a platform erected on 'execution days' outside the prison itself, a ritual attended by large and often drunken and unruly crowds.

In February 1807, twenty-eight onlookers were crushed to death when a cart on which some were standing in the hope of having a better view of the execution collapsed, many of them being trampled as others scrambled to mount what remained of the cart for a better view of the execution. More than a century was to pass before hanging was abolished in England.

FINAL DAYS

In 1868, in an attempt to end such scenes, executions were moved inside the prison to the execution chamber. Between that date and the demolition of Newgate in 1902, 49 women and 1,106 men met their deaths within the prison walls, more than in any other prison. After 1880, use of the prison was gradually discontinued and demolition began on 15 August 1902 to make room for the expansion of its neighbour, the Old Bailey.

An auction was held of some of the prison's more exotic contents. The black flag which was raised following an execution was sold to a South African for 11½ guineas (just over £12) and the purchaser's descendants presumably still own it, though one wonders for what purpose they use it. The bell which was tolled on the occasion of an execution was sold to Madame Tussauds waxworks museum for £100, where it took up residence in the museum's Chamber of Horrors.

The scaffold and other materials associated with executions were removed to Pentonville Prison where they remained in use for almost sixty years, its victims there including the Irish patriot Roger Casement, the murderer Dr Hawley Crippen and Edwin Bush, the last to be hanged there on 6 July 1961, having been convicted of stabbing to death a 59-year-old shop assistant.

3

JUDGES
AND MEN OF STRAW

TRIAL BY JURY

The use of juries can be traced back to the years before 1066 and were prominent in the reign of Henry II (1154–89), when groups of local citizens in what came to be called Grand Juries were employed to put local criminals before the king's judges and present evidence against them. They later developed into bodies which heard preliminary evidence in criminal matters and decided whether there was a case to answer. They still do this for certain cases in the USA, though their use in Great Britain ceased in 1933, the task falling instead to magistrates. By 1222 petty juries were being used as they are now, to decide guilt or innocence in criminal cases, thus fulfilling the requirement of Clause 39 of Magna Carta of 1215.

'YOU HAVE THE BODY'

It was underpinned by the writ of *habeas corpus* ('you have the body') which, when issued by a court, requires the authorities (e.g. the police) to deliver an arrested person to a court. Charles I tried to circumvent the process in his disputes with Parliament, and in 1679 it was enshrined in law in the Habeas Corpus Act. It means, in practice, that an arrested person cannot be kept in custody for more than 48 hours without being presented to court.

This is why Magistrates' Courts sit on Saturday mornings, since a person arrested on Friday evening cannot be kept in the cells until Monday morning.

SUMMARY JUSTICE

The expression 'summary justice' has a very different meaning in the twenty-first century from that which applied in earlier times. Its present usage refers to justice as dispensed in magistrates' courts which deal with 'summary offences'. Most motoring offences, drunken and disorderly behaviour and many others including, curiously, assaulting a police officer, are dealt with exclusively in magistrates' courts, normally by a bench of three lay magistrates advised by a legally qualified court clerk.

Magistrates are holders of an ancient office, also known as Justices of the Peace (JPs). They are first mentioned in the Justices of the Peace Statute of 1361, an Act which clearly refers to an already existing office dating back, probably, to the reign of Richard I (1189–99). There are about 25,000 such magistrates, who deal with about 95 per cent of all criminal cases, the remaining 5 per cent (murder, rape, armed robbery, serious violence, etc.) being sent by magistrates to the Crown Courts for trial by a judge and jury.

Magistrates are not paid and until well into the nineteenth century, they performed most of the functions of local government outside towns as well as sitting in courts. They were (and are) a very cost-effective way for the government to administer the system of justice. Nowadays magistrates do not sit on cases involving people they know for good or ill, but in medieval times most justices were local gentry who knew the local villains and could round them up and keep them in the local gaol or bridewell prior to trial. The name bridewell is derived from Henry VIII's palace of that name near Blackfriars, named after St Bridget, which was given by Edward VI to the City as a house of correction for unruly apprentices.

In earlier times the expression 'summary justice' had a less reassuring meaning and referred to the speed with which cases were heard and sentences carried out, often at the expense of justice. This explains why, in Shakespeare's *King Henry VI Part 2*, in response to Jack Cade's extravagant promises of good times for all, his fellow rebel Dick replies, 'The first thing we do, let's kill all the lawyers.'

THE OLD BAILEY: OPEN JUSTICE

The Old Bailey is mentioned in records in the reign of Elizabeth I, though it probably dates from the rebuilding of the adjacent gaol of Newgate under the will of Richard Whittington in the previous century. It was originally called the Middlesex Sessions House and was intended for the trials of those accused of crimes in the City of London and Middlesex, other defendants being tried in their local areas. In 1834 it was renamed the Central Criminal Court and its jurisdiction was extended to cover serious crimes throughout England and Wales.

Most serious criminal trials are still held in local Crown Courts (formerly known as assizes since the reign of Henry II) but in 1856 the trial of the Staffordshire poisoner, Dr William Palmer, set a precedent for the most notorious and controversial trials when Palmer's case was transferred to the Old Bailey in the belief that he could not have a fair trial in his native county. The Old Bailey has often featured in fiction. In *A Tale of Two Cities*, Charles Darnay's trial takes place at the Old Bailey and John Mortimer's creation Horace Rumpole pursues his faltering legal career there in *Rumpole of the Bailey*. Like its neighbour Newgate Prison, the building was destroyed in the Great Fire of 1666 and rebuilt on part of its present site. Given the insalubrious nature of its work (and indeed of many of its users), the new court was open to the weather to inhibit the spread of disease: a novel example of open justice!

In 1734 the building was enclosed in order to reduce the influence of spectators whose raucous comments did nothing to add to the dignity of its proceedings, but this probably helped the typhus to spread. In an attempt to prevent further deaths from the foul

air the practice developed of placing sprigs of rue, also known as
'herb of grace', before the dock. This was an aromatic herb whose
pungent smell would, it was hoped, mask the worst effects of the
polluted air. In 1849, following the conviction of Frederick and
Marie Manning for the murder of Marie's lover, the lady was so
enraged by the proceedings that she picked up the springs of rue
'and threw them vehemently over the wigged heads of the learned
gentlemen'. The missiles didn't help her case and they were the first
married couple to be executed together since 1700.

Dr William Palmer.

NO BLINDFOLD

The Old Bailey was rebuilt again at the same time as Newgate, following the Gordon Riots of 1780, and a second courtroom was added in 1824, taking over the site of the adjacent Surgeons' Hall, which was relocated

The Central Criminal Court, better known as the Old Bailey.

to its present site in Lincoln's Inn Fields. The present court building, occupying also the site of the former Newgate Prison, was opened in 1907. It was severely damaged by bombing during the Blitz and rebuilt in the 1950s, its interior decorated by phrases of legal axioms, statues of royalty and legal figures and paintings commemorating the Blitz. It had nineteen courts, one of them used as a press room and the rest for trials. The dome of the building is surmounted by the female figure of Lady Justice holding scales (to weigh the evidence) and a sword (to administer justice). Contrary to popular belief, the figure is not blindfolded. The Old Bailey survived an attempt by the Provisional IRA to blow it up in 1973.

JUDGES

The Old Bailey judges include some unusual people:

The Lord Mayor for many years sat as a judge at the Old Bailey, despite his lack of legal qualifications. This role derived from the fact that in the reign of King John (1199–1216), the citizens of London, in return for a payment to the king, were given the right to elect their own chief magistrate (i.e the mayor). The first mayor was Henry Fitzalwyn. Appointed (not elected) in 1189, he remained in office for twenty-four years. The present term of office is one year and no one has approached Fitzalwyn's record. The term *Domino majori* (loosely translated as lord mayor) is first recorded in 1283 and in 1545 the title Lord Mayor came into use, though it has never been officially conferred.

The Sheriffs of London hold the most ancient office in the City, having been first appointed in 1132. In the shires the sheriffs, or shire-reeves, were 'country justices' responsible for the routine administration of the laws and thus held judicial offices.

The Court of Aldermen was established by King John in 1200 and was the governing body of the City, a function now discharged by the Court of Common Council. The court's functions are now mainly ceremonial. Aldermen are ex officio Justices of the Peace for the City of London Magistrates' Court, which is adjacent to the Mansion House.

All of the above are entitled to sit on the judges' bench of the Old Bailey, but may play no part in the proceedings. Traditionally, the presiding judge sits slightly off-centre on the bench in recognition of the fact that the Lord Mayor may choose to sit, in which case he would occupy the central position. In practice, the Lord Mayor does not exercise this right. Neither do the sheriffs or aldermen.

The Recorder of London is the most senior judge sitting at the Old Bailey, though the term 'recorder' normally indicates a relatively junior part-time judge sitting occasionally in Crown Courts to deal with crimes or County Courts for civil actions between individuals. The office of Recorder of London is an ancient one, dating from 1298, and the role has been filled by many distinguished judges such as Sir Edward Coke (1552–1634) and one notorious one, Judge Jeffreys (1645–89).

The Common Serjeant of London is the deputy to the Recorder, the office dating from 1319. Like the Recorder, the Serjeant is technically elected by aldermen, but since 1888 has been appointed to his judicial office by the Crown. Judge Jeffreys also

You wouldn't expect much mercy from this grim pair.

served as Common Serjeant, as did Mervyn Griffith Jones (1909–79), who is chiefly remembered for asking the jury in the *Lady Chatterley's Lover* trial whether they would want their servants or wives to read the offending work of literature.

The Lord Chancellor is ex officio, a judge of the Old Bailey, as is the Lord Chief Justice and all judges of the High Court. All judges in the Old Bailey, regardless of rank, are addressed as 'My Lord' or 'My Lady'. On certain occasions, judges of the Old Bailey carry posies or 'nosegays' of flowers, a reminder of the days when the foul air from Newgate Prison next door and from the crowds in the court itself made breathing unpleasant.

An account of the Old Bailey's work, published in 1868, describes the various roles of the Lord Mayor, aldermen and others, and went on to explain that 'a judge of the law only assists when unusual points of the law are involved or when conviction affects the life of the prisoner', suggesting a rather casual approach to the administration of justice at the time!

SOME FAMOUS DEFENDANTS

Given its prominent place in the English legal system, it is not surprising that the Old Bailey has witnessed the trials of some of the most prominent and infamous defendants to pass through the judicial system.

Oscar Wilde (1854–1900). In 1895 Wilde was accused by the Marquess of Queensberry of 'posing as a somdomite' [*sic*, spelling was not one of Queensberry's strengths], whereupon Wilde rashly prosecuted him for libel. The marquess produced evidence of the author's homosexual activities, which were illegal back then. Wilde's case collapsed and he was in turn prosecuted for sodomy and gross indecency. In his first trial the jury was unable to agree on a verdict, but a second trial produced a verdict of guilty and Wilde was sentenced to two years' hard labour. His reputation never recovered and after his release Wilde died in poverty in Paris in 1900.

Oscar Wilde, before his fall from grace.

Dr Hawley Crippen (1862–1910) was an American physician who moved to England in 1897 with his promiscuous actress wife Cora and practised as a purveyor of patent and homeopathic medicines, his medical qualifications not being recognised in England. In 1910 his wife disappeared and a search of their house revealed human remains. In the meantime, Crippen and his lover Ethel Neve had fled to America. The captain of the SS *Montrose*, on which the pair were travelling, telegraphed his suspicions to London and Inspector Dew of Scotland Yard boarded a faster vessel, arresting Crippen as he landed in Canada. Crippen was found guilty of the murder of his wife and hanged at Pentonville on 23 November 1910, on the scaffold removed from Newgate ten years earlier.

George Joseph Smith (1872–1915) the Brides in the Bath murderer, conducted a number of bigamous marriages using aliases to conceal his identity. He then drowned three women to whom he was bigamously married by pulling their legs up while they were in the bath, suddenly submerging their heads. The evidence of the celebrated pathologist Sir Bernard Spilsbury (1877–1947) was instrumental in securing Smith's conviction and he was hanged in Maidstone Prison on 13 August 1913.

William Joyce ('Lord Haw-Haw', 1906–46) was an Irish-American Nazi sympathiser who made propaganda broadcasts to Britain during the Second World War, his nickname deriving from his mirthless laugh. There were doubts about the validity of the charge of high treason, given his foreign nationality, but he was convicted on the grounds that he had acquired a British passport, albeit by giving false information. He was hanged on 3 January 1946 at Wandsworth Prison.

Neville Heath (1917–46), after a troubled but sometimes heroic wartime record in the South African Air Force, murdered two young women for no apparent reason, and savagely mutilated their bodies. He pleaded not guilty by reason of insanity but was found guilty and executed on 16 October 1946 at Pentonville. Offered a whisky before the execution, he replied, 'Make it a double.' Heath had dated the actress Moira Lister in the summer of 1946 and his motives for the murders remain a mystery.

John Christie (1899–1953) was a petty criminal who murdered eight women, one of them his wife, by strangling them at his lodgings at 10 Rillington Place, Notting Hill. The bodies were discovered after he moved out and after an innocent man, Timothy Evans, had been wrongly convicted of the murder of Evans's daughter, for which he was hanged. Christie was convicted in the same courtroom in which Timothy Evans had appeared, with Christie as a prosecution witness. Christie pleaded insanity but was convicted and hanged on 15 July 1953 at Pentonville by the famous hangman Albert Pierrepoint who had earlier hanged the luckless Evans.

Peter Sutcliffe ('The Yorkshire Ripper', born 1946) murdered thirteen women and attempted to murder seven others in the West Riding of Yorkshire between 1969 and 1980. He appears to have been motivated by hatred of prostitutes (whose services he used), though many of his victims were respectable women. The hunt for him was distracted by a number of false leads, including a tape recording from the supposed culprit who turned out to be a hoaxer nicknamed Wearside Jack. Sutcliffe was convicted of all thirteen murders, the judge having rejected a plea of guilty to manslaughter due to diminished responsibility. Sutcliffe was eventually sentenced to a whole life term and is at present in Broadmoor, diagnosed with paranoid schizophrenia. He has been attacked on a number of occasions while detained. 'Wearside Jack' (John Humble) was convicted of perverting the course of justice on the strength of DNA evidence on an envelope and sentenced to eight years in 2006.

MEN OF STRAW

Proceedings in criminal trials, most notably at the Old Bailey, were greatly expedited by the Men of Straw. These were men who loitered in the vicinity of the courthouse with pieces of straw protruding from their pockets and shoes as a signal that they were prepared to give evidence for whichever party was prepared to pay them. Others did it from motives of mutual assistance. One such person was described by the novelist and magistrate Henry Fielding, who turned Bow Street Magistrates' Court from a den of corruption to a haven of justice. Fielding wrote that 'The usual defence of a thief, especially at the Old Bailey, is an alibi. To prove this by perjury is a common act of Newgate friendship and there seldom is any difficulty procuring such witnesses. I remember a felon to have been proved to be in Ireland at the time when the robbery was sworn to have been done in London, and acquitted; but he was scarce gone from the bar when the witness was himself arrested for a robbery in London at that very time when he swore both he and his friend were in Dublin; for which robbery he was tried and executed.'

BEEFSTEAKS AND REFRACTORY JURIES

In 1830 a quack doctor called St John Long was prosecuted at the Old Bailey for the manslaughter of one of his patients, a trial which was notable for the behaviour of the judges. The trial took place on a Saturday and the presiding judge, Mr Justice Park, retired to dinner at about 5 p.m., having directed that the jury, who were having difficulty in agreeing upon a verdict, be locked up during the meal. In the words of a contemporary account, 'The dinner proceeded merrily, the beef-steaks were renewed again and again and received the solemn sanction of judicial approval repeatedly. The chaplain was on the point of being challenged for a song when the court-keeper appeared with a face of consternation to announce that the jury had fallen into a dull, dead lull'. The jury couldn't agree. Mr Justice Park, who was 'a warm admirer of the times when refractory juries were carried round the country in a cart declared his intention of waiting till what he deemed a reasonable hour and then informing the jury that if they were not agreed they must be locked up without fire or candle until a reasonable hour on the

A predecessor of Horace Rumpole.

Monday by which time he trusted they would be unanimous.' St John Long was found guilty shortly afterwards and fined £150. He died four years later and was buried in the Harrow Road Cemetery, his tomb marked by a monument bearing an inscription which recorded the gratitude of his many satisfied patients.

'STOP HIS MOUTH'

Long's case was not the first time a judge had put pressure on a jury. In 1667 the Quaker William Penn held a meeting of the Society of Friends (as the Quakers are properly called) in Gracechurch Street in the heart of the City after their meeting house was closed by the authorities, who were worried by the dissident religious views of this harmless and pacifist group of citizens. Penn was tried at the Old Bailey before a bench which included the Lord Mayor, the curious charge claiming that he had 'met together with force of arms to the terror and disturbance of His Majesty's subjects'. Penn's sharp mind enabled him to expose the absurdity of this charge, whereupon the Lord Mayor cried, 'Stop his mouth! Bring fetters and stake him to the ground.' The jury, who agreed with Penn, returned a verdict of 'not guilty', whereupon the enraged Lord Mayor shouted, 'You shall not be dismissed till we have a verdict that the court will accept. You will be locked up without meat, drink, fire or tobacco. We will have a verdict by the Grace of God or you shall starve for it.' The jury were locked up in Newgate but remained resolute, even in the face of further threats and fines from the Lord Mayor. They were eventually released under a writ of *habeas corpus* and a decision by the Lord Chief Justice that jurors could not be coerced or punished for their verdicts.

A WELL-FED CHAPLAIN

The dinner which Mr Justice Park did not wish to interrupt was a traditional feature of the work of the Old Bailey which continued until the 1830s. The City Sheriffs provided the dinners for the judges and for the aldermen, other City grandees and a few members of the Bar. The first course varied with the season but the main course invariably involved beefsteaks. Two identical dinners were served each day; the first at 3 p.m. and the second at 5 p.m. The work of the judges meant that each could attend only one dinner, but the aldermen and the chaplain frequently attended both. According to a contemporary account, 'This invaluable public servant persevered from a sheer sense of duty, till he had acquired the habit of eating two dinners a day, and practised it for nearly ten years without any perceptible injury to his health. We had the pleasure of witnessing his performances at one of the five o'clock dinners, and can assert with confidence, that the vigour of his attack on the beef-steaks was wholly unimpaired by the effective execution a friend assured us he had done on them two hours before.'

AIR CONDITIONING, VICTORIAN STYLE

In 1841, mindful of the deaths from typhus which had occurred in the previous century in the adjoining Newgate Prison, the Old Bailey installed a ventilation system designed by a Dr David Reid. This was the same Dr David Reid who had designed a heating and ventilation system for the Palace of Westminster, which was at the time being rebuilt following the Great Fire of 1834. The fire had started in the medieval heating system when it was fed with rotting wooden tally sticks, which had been used to record payments of taxes since the reign of Henry I. The entire building had been destroyed except for Westminster Hall. Charles Barry, the much vilified architect of the new palace, had demonstrated that the system proposed for Westminster by Reid would probably have produced a similar conflagration upon its first use, so Reid was dismissed from his job at the Palace of Westminster and turned his attentions instead to the Old Bailey. Perhaps he had been chastened by Barry's criticisms because the Old Bailey survived Reid's elaborate system of subterranean tunnels, fans, chambers and cowls which, together with other sanitary measures, protected lawyers, jurymen and criminals alike from the horrors of typhus.

4

WHO'D LIKE TO BE A GAOLER?

KEEPING A PRIVATE PRISON

In the twenty-first century we are accustomed to the idea that gaols might be run by private companies for profit, but there is nothing novel about it. Before the prison reforms of John Howard (1726–1790) and Elizabeth Fry (1780–1845), there was no expectation that the government would involve itself in the management of prisons, either at national or local level. The role of national government was to defend the kingdom and to administer the courts, much of the latter work being carried out (as it still is) by unpaid magistrates who were also responsible for the rudimentary local government that took place outside towns. It was not until the reign of Queen Victoria (1837–1901) that government began to involve itself in such measures as education, public health and prisons.

Prior to that time prisons were, in effect, regarded as a source of revenue. Prison sentences following trials were unusual. As indicated earlier, fines, floggings, humiliation like the stocks and pillory, transportation and executions were the normal penalties. Prisons were designed to hold criminals for relatively short periods before their trials, and the people most likely to be found in prison for longer periods were debtors who had been locked up at the request of their creditors. Prisons, whether for criminals or debtors (and most prisons contained some of each) were run by keepers who had purchased the post from a government agency, rather like a franchise, and were expected to earn back their outlay, and more besides, by exactions on the prisoners in their care.

WATERING THE PRISON BEER

It was normal for a prison to be divided between a Masters' side and a Commons' side. In the Masters' side conditions could be pleasant, with good food, beer, wine, a comfortable bed, a degree of privacy and access to visitors, including prostitutes. Some favoured and wealthy prisoners could even stay in the keeper's own quarters. In 1730 a prisoner called Joseph Woolan and his wife discovered that, in the absence of any regulations governing the provision of victuals, there was nothing to stop them opening their own bar. The keeper, enraged, had this enterprise banned by the City Sheriff, though this official did not always take the side of the keeper. Some years later, following a complaint that the keeper's beer had been watered down, the sheriff ordered that the prisoners be reimbursed.

IRON COLLARS

The Commons' side could be a place of filth, privation and squalor, ridden with typhus (or gaol fever) which was transmitted from person to person by fleas. It was very common in prisons and, as we have seen, sometimes affected the courts themselves (as in the outbreak at the Old Bailey in 1750). It was in the interests of the keepers to encourage as many inmates as possible to reside in the Masters' side of the prison, where fees could be exacted, and the prisoners were encouraged to make this choice from the moment of their arrival. The process was described by a garden designer and writer called Batty Langley, who was sent to Newgate in 1724 for a debt and left an account of his reception. Prisoners arriving from the courts would commonly have manacles and shackles on the wrists and ankles and iron collars around their necks. Langley described how the irons would remain in place until the victims paid 'easement' to have them removed. One prisoner, who either couldn't or wouldn't pay, died when a neck iron was fastened so tightly that it broke his spine. It was in the interests of the keepers to have as many prisoners as possible, so one Newgate keeper paid £40 per annum to Sir Francis Mitchell, a Justice of the Peace for Middlesex, in return for which all Mitchell's prisoners were sent to Newgate.

PLEADING A BELLY

Besides the division between Masters' and Commons', the larger prisons also had separate accommodation for felons who had committed serious criminal offences and for debtors; and again separate quarters for men and women though in 1700 the Keeper of Newgate, William Robison, charged male prisoners 6*d* for admission to the women's quarters. The women often welcomed this, not least because, if a woman became pregnant, she could 'plead her belly' and escape a death sentence.

A SPOT OF GARNISH

Those who, like Batty Langley, were admitted to the Masters' side of the debtors' section paid 6*s* 6*d* (32.5p) for admission and 10*s* 6*d* (52.5p) for 'garnish', which entitled them to a supply of coal and candles. In the Marshalsea this 'garnish' gave access to the kitchen for boiling water and preparing meals and also secured a supply of newspapers. The new prisoner would then be given a 'chum ticket' which allocated him a room, normally shared with another prisoner, though wealthier prisoners could have rooms for themselves or their families for an additional 2*s* 6*d* (12.5p) a week. Prisoners who defaulted on their garnish payments were humiliated: their names were called out by the prison crier and written on a board in the kitchen, and no one spoke to them.

NO SMOKING IN THE BEER ROOM

The process was administered by a committee of prisoners who were elected by the inmates. In the Marshalsea the committee

numbered nine and was for a while chaired by John Dickens, father
to Charles, meeting every Monday at 11 a.m. They imposed fines for
unruly behaviour, urinating in the yard, defacing the walls, smoking
in the beer room at inappropriate times or a variety of other
offences. Some prisoners adjusted to the routine, which removed
the ever-present threat of creditors and bailiffs, as Dr Haggage in
Little Dorrit explains to another prisoner:

> We are quiet here; we don't get badgered here; there's no
> knocker to be hammered at by creditors. Nobody comes here
> to ask if a man's home and to say he'll stand on the doormat
> until he is. Nobody writes threatening letters about money
> to this place. It's freedom sir, it's freedom. We have got to the
> bottom, we can't fall and what have we found? Peace.

Debtors were sometimes relieved to be sent to the Masters' side
of a prison like the Marshalsea if they were thereby released from
a sponging house, so called because they squeezed the debtor like
a sponge to extract the maximum payment from him. These were
usually run by bailiffs, where the inmates were grossly overcharged
for food, wine, tobacco and other essentials. Batty Langley estimated
that a day in the sponging house had cost him ten times as much as a
day in reasonable comfort on the Masters' Side in Newgate.

'STRIPPED, BEATEN AND ABUSED'

Life was not so pleasant for those on the Commons' side who could
not afford the gaolers' demands. In the words of a contemporary
account, those 'not having the wherewithal to pay were stripped,
beaten and abused in a most violent manner'. Batty Langley wrote of
the Commons' side in Newgate that 'such wickedness abounds therein
that the place seems to have the exact aspect of Hell itself'. There were
no beds, food was of the poorest quality and was often charged for,
even if it had been given to the prison by a charity. Those who couldn't
pay starved. The prisoners were supervised by 'cellarmen', who were
themselves prisoners appointed by the keepers to distribute food and
maintain order. Sometimes the cellarmen sold food which had been
donated for the prisoners by shopkeepers. If prisoners were unwilling

to make payments that the cellarmen reckoned they could afford, then they could be placed in a room through which the prison sewer flowed and in which corpses of deceased prisoners were kept overnight. That usually had the desired effect.

FIVE-STAR ACCOMMODATION

The most salubrious accommodation in Newgate was, paradoxically, the press yard, where people had previously been pressed to death but which, by Langley's time, had fallen into disuse. Fees for admission to this five-star accommodation which offered the facilities of a comfortable home could be as much as £500. A cleaner was available for a 1s a week and a prostitute cost 1s a night. One privileged occupant described how, in 1715, he was welcomed into the press yard by a young man called George who had been gaoled for wearing his best suit on the birthday of the 'Old Pretender King James III', who had led an uprising against the Hanoverian monarchy that year. The press yard had the atmosphere of a gentlemen's club, many of his companions being army officers who had backed the wrong side in the struggle between the Stuarts and the Hanoverians, while there was also an orange merchant, a mathematician and a classical scholar. One evening their conversation was enlivened by a visit from the executioner, who was speculating on the money he would make from executing those who had joined the Old Pretender's rebellion and from selling their clothes. The going rate, he informed his audience, was £3 for beheading a peer and the same for hanging, drawing and quartering a gentleman. They must have been impressed! The keeper of Newgate, whose name was Pitt, had paid £5,000 for the office, so the 1715 rebellion was a great stroke of luck for him since he made an estimated £4,000 from fees arising from the rebellion alone: an excellent return.

THE CONDEMNED SERMON

A further source of income was the condemned sermon. Executions at Tyburn were usually carried out on Mondays so the previous evening the Newgate chaplain, known as the Newgate Ordinary, would preach the condemned sermon to those prisoners who were to be executed the following morning and who sat in the condemned pew. To remind them of their imminent fate, a coffin would be laid in the middle of the chapel. The condemned services were very popular with the local population, who would pay

The condemned cell, Newgate.

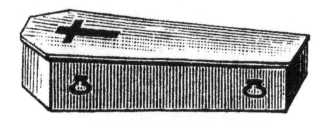

handsomely to be admitted to them, for the privilege of watching the condemned prisoners both at the service and afterwards in the condemned cell. Decorum was not a feature of these services. In 1716 one Ordinary complained that prisoners were using the communion table for eating and drinking and in 1719 disruption followed when a prisoner smuggled a bawdy pamphlet into the service in his hat and circulated it amongst his fellow prisoners.

'OLD BAILEY LADIES'

The service, and particularly the condemned sermon itself, would habitually be interrupted by visitors commenting upon the demeanour of those about to die and quibbling with the gaolers over the prices of admission to this unusual religious observance. A good service, with well-known prisoners, could easily yield a profit of £20 to the gaolers, the prices varying according to the demand. Many of these visitors were what *Punch* called 'Old Bailey Ladies', regular attenders who, in the words of the magazine, 'attended these macabre events in order to have their Christianity and their morals mightily refreshed.' It compared the entertainments at Newgate with the more mundane pleasures of the theatre: 'Who would seek the vulgar playhouse when, with Newgate interest, ladies may be on the free list for all condemned sermons, when they may witness real agony, may behold a real murderer writhing in all the hell of horror and despair.'

BEATEN WITH A BULL'S PIZZLE

Some keepers were more brutal than others in their exactions and treatment of prisoners. In 1330 Edmund Lorimer, Keeper of Newgate, was sent to Fleet Prison for torturing prisoners, and one of his predecessors was hanged for murdering one of those in his care. In 1393 the Court of Aldermen of the City of London set a maximum charge of £5 (still a huge sum) for removing irons. In 1729 William Acton, a butcher, and Thomas Bambridge, who had purchased the Keeperships of the Marshalsea and the Fleet respectively, were tried for mistreatment of prisoners in their charge. Acton was charged with the murder of Thomas Bliss, a debtor who had been unable to pay Acton for food and tried to escape. Acton had beaten him with a bull's pizzle (penis), stamped on him and placed him in a room in which he could not lie down or stand up. Bliss was left there for three weeks wearing a head vice, thumb screws, an iron collar and leg and hand irons. Bliss died and similar accounts were given on behalf of other prisoners. Acton was acquitted on the testimony of some of his more favoured prisoners, and because the government did not want it to become known that Acton had purchased the Keepership illegally. Bambridge, about whom similar evidence was given, was not so lucky. He was sent to Newgate Prison and forbidden to enjoy the proceeds of the office of keeper, for which, like Acton, he had paid £5,000.

Perhaps private prison operators like G4S aren't such a bad lot after all.

5

GO TO GAOL.
AND STAY
THERE!

THE MARSHALSEA

Just off Borough High Street in Southwark, south of Guy's Hospital, is a short passage now called Angel Place, known to Charles Dickens as Angel Court. For him it held dark memories as a place of shame for his family. His parents had been held in the Marshalsea Debtors' Prison (of which Angel Place is the surviving remnant) while the young Charles, at the age of 12, had been sent to work in Warren's blacking factory. There he wrapped bottles of shoe polish, close to the present site of Charing Cross Station. John Dickens owed the substantial sum of £40 to a baker and spent three months in the Marshalsea. Charles found lodgings in nearby Lant Street so that he could take breakfast with his family before going to work and then dine with them afterwards. He gave his most vivid description of the Marshalsea in his novel *Little Dorrit*, the family of that name being incarcerated there for so long that, upon release, they were unable to cope with the world. The family's fate is due to an uncompleted contract with the Circumlocution Office, a biting satire on the processes of the law:

> Thirty years ago there stood the Marshalsea Prison, a few
> doors short of the church of Saint George, in the Borough of
> Southwark, on the left hand side of the way going southward.

It had stood there many years before and it remained there some years afterwards, but it is gone now and the world is none the worse without it.

Besides Angel Place, one can also find nearby Marshalsea Road and Little Dorrit Court, and in Angel Place itself there is a plaque fixed to the wall which once marked the southern boundary of the prison. The buildings of the Marshalsea were sold to an ironmonger after its closure in 1842 and, although most of the site was redeveloped later in the century, a small part survived as a hardware store for George Harding and Sons into the 1950s. Now only the southern wall remains.

PIRATES, DEBTORS AND THE HEADMASTER OF ETON

The Marshalsea was one of several debtors' prisons in London and elsewhere which existed to hold people who owed money to others. The Marshalsea owed its name to the marshal of the king's household. who was in theory its governor. It dated from the fourteenth century or earlier and in its early days dealt with offences committed on the high seas and a variety of other crimes in the Tudor period. Roman Catholics suspected of sedition were sent there, along with Shakespeare's contemporary Ben Jonson, who was gaoled there in 1597 for a play called *The Isle of Dogs* which was considered so seditious that all copies of the offending work were destroyed, so it is lost to history. In 1541 a headmaster of Eton was sent there for buggery, though the fact that he was later appointed as headmaster of Westminster suggests that he was forgiven. The Fleet Prison was another debtor's prison, even older, dating from 1197 and situated at the bottom of Fleet Street, off the Farringdon road. Under the Insolvent Debtors' Act of 1813, debtors could seek release after two weeks in prison by declaring that their assets did not exceed £20, but if any one creditor objected they had to remain in prison. The debtors' prisons were abolished in 1869 by the Debtors' Act of that year, though debtors who had the means to pay off their creditors but chose not to do so could still be imprisoned for up to six weeks.

MASTERS' AND COMMONS'

The Marshalsea, like Newgate, was divided into the Masters' side where prisoners (albeit debtors) paid to live in considerable comfort, and the Commons' side where they lived in squalor. Those on the Masters' side who could afford to pay the governor for their accommodation could have private rooms, access to a coffee shop, a chandler's, a tailor and a barber. There was also a chophouse run by Richard McDonell and his wife. The chophouse was called Titty Doll's, presumably a reference to the famous gingerbread maker Tiddy Doll, who attended executions at Tyburn with his wares. One can understand the frustration of those to whom the debtors owed money who saw them living at ease. The Commons' side could see prisoners held thirty or more to a rat-infested room with little or no food or fresh water. Since the governors had purchased the right to run the prison from the king's marshal, they had every incentive to make conditions in the Commons' side unpleasant in order to encourage the residents to move to the profitable, fee-paying Masters' side. Further payments allowed inmates to conduct business, receive visitors and even live outside the prison, a process known as the Liberty of the Fleet.

FLEET MARRIAGES

Another peculiarity of the Fleet Prison was the Fleet marriage, which was conducted outside the home parish of the spouses, without the reading of banns and usually against the wishes of the families of the bride and groom. The Fleet Prison claimed to be outside the jurisdiction of the church and Fleet marriages were profitable both for the gaolers and for the clergymen who conducted them. It has been estimated that in the 1740s more than one in eight marriages in the whole of England took place in the vicinity of the Fleet Prison, conducted by up to 100 clergymen. These ceased after the passing of the 1753 Marriage Act, which declared null and void any marriage conducted without banns being read in the local parish, and made any clergyman who officiated in such a marriage liable to transportation.

In February 1729 James Oglethorpe, a Member of Parliament, was alarmed by the death of a friend in the Fleet Prison. His friend, who had refused to pay a higher fee to the manager of the Fleet Prison, was placed in a cell with a man dying of smallpox to which he duly succumbed. Oglethorpe formed a Parliamentary Gaols Committee and visited the prison where they found a baronet, Sir William Rich, held in irons, beaten and burned with a red hot poker and kept in a dungeon for ten days. They also found prisoners being starved to death. They found similar conditions in the Marshalsea, where 300 inmates had starved to death in three months, with ten dying every day in warm weather. However, when the governors of each establishment were put on trial they were found not guilty on all charges; a guilty verdict would have reflected badly on the marshall who had sold the offices to the brutal governors. Oglethorpe later founded the colony of Georgia in North America as a settlement colony for debtors who were unable to put their affairs in order.

MR MICAWBER

In 1811 the Marshalsea was refurbished and thereafter used exclusively for debtors who, besides the family of Dickens, also included Sir Marc Brunel, inventor and father of the engineer Isambard Kingdom Brunel. Marc's debts were due to the fact that the admiralty failed to pay him for an invention: he was released when he threatened to sell his invention (for making ships' blocks for guiding ropes on warships) to the Tsar of Russia. The belated payment of £5,000 enabled him to secure his release and, with the balance, re-establish himself as a successful entrepreneur. Other inmates included Nelson's paramour Emma Hamilton and the poets Christopher Smart and John Donne, as well as the fictional Wilkins Micawber in *David Copperfield*. According to David's account, it was in the Marshalsea that Micawber recorded his most famous observation:

Mr Micawber was waiting for me within the gate and we went up to his room (top storey but one) and cried very much. He solemnly conjured me to take warning by his fate; and to observe that if a man had twenty pounds a year for his income and spent nineteen pounds nineteen shillings and sixpence he would be happy but that if he spent twenty pounds one he would be miserable. After which he borrowed a shilling off me for porter.

Wilkins Micawber's character, and in particular his inability to manage his financial affairs, owes much to Charles Dickens's father John, with whom Charles enjoyed an affectionate but far from respectful relationship. The character of Samuel Pickwick was also gaoled for debt, for breach of promise in *Pickwick Papers*, as, of course, was also Sir John Falstaff in *Henry IV Part II*, of whom the Chief Justice says, 'Go, carry Sir John Falstaff to the Fleet; take all his company along with him.'

A BET THAT WENT WRONG

Besides the Marshalsea and the Fleet, there were other smaller prisons also used for debtors and other minor criminals. These were called compters, of which the best known was the Poultry Compter in the small street which runs from the Bank of England to Cheapside, and took its name from the produce sold in its street market. Besides debtors there were some stranger inmates, including a man who was arrested in July 1799 for being found naked outside the Mansion House. He had bet £10 that he could run naked from Cornhill to Cheapside.

'THE MAIDEN TRIBUTE OF MODERN BABYLON'

The Poultry Compter also found a small place in the struggle against slavery when, in 1765, an abolitionist called Granville Sharp learned that a freed slave had been apprehended at the request of his former owner and confined in the Poultry Compter. Upon appeal to the Lord Mayor, the slave, John Strong, was released and found employment with an apothecary. Coldbath Fields Prison also housed debtors. It was first constructed in the reign of James I (1603–25) and took its name from Coldbath Spring in Clerkenwell. It was at one time London's largest prison with 2,000 inmates, of whom the most notable was the editor of *The Pall Mall Gazette*, W.T. Stead, who was gaoled after publishing a series of articles called 'The Maiden Tribute of Modern Babylon' which revealed how easy it was to purchase a young girl. Stead had agreed the 'purchase' of the child, 13-year-old Eliza Armstrong, for £5 with her mother and placed Eliza in the care of the Salvation Army. The articles caused a great scandal and led to the age of consent being raised from 13 to 16 but Stead, who had caused great embarrassment to the authorities, was gaoled on a technicality (he had the mother's permission to purchase Eliza but not the father's), and emerged a hero after a three-month sentence. Thereafter he always wore his prison uniform each year on the anniversary of his sentence and later died on the *Titanic* after helping others into lifeboats. George Bernard Shaw was moved by Stead's articles to write *Pygmalion* and named the principal character, Eliza Doolittle, after Eliza Armstrong. Coldbath Fields Prison closed in 1885, soon after Stead's release, and its former site is now occupied by the Royal Mail's Mount Pleasant sorting office.

Debtors' prisons were never popular. The Fleet was destroyed by Wat Tyler's men during the Peasants' Revolt in 1381 and again by the Gordon Rioters in 1780. When the Fleet Prison closed in 1842, some prisoners were found to have been there for thirty years.

6

GET OUT OF GAOL FREE CARD

HENRY HAD A POINT

Few people (apart from those wise enough to read this book) know that Henry II was the father of the Common Law. Some people know that he had a foul temper. Most people remember him as the king who was held responsible for the death of Thomas Becket, Archbishop of Canterbury, murdered in his cathedral on 29 December 1170 by four knights who thought they were doing the king's bidding. Becket's death turned him into a saint, established Canterbury as a place of pilgrimage to rival Rome and Santiago de Compostela in Spain and inspired both Chaucer's greatest work *The Canterbury Tales* and T.S. Eliot's *Murder in the Cathedral*. Hardly anyone knows that, in his dispute with his troublesome priest, Henry had a point that was eventually resolved to the advantage of later monarchs. How did this come about?

CLARENDON

South-east of Salisbury is Clarendon Palace, now a ruin, though even in its present state it is clear that it was once a magnificent building. It was the principal royal residence in the west of England, situated in the royal forest of Clarendon, and remained a royal property until it was confiscated by Parliament following the civil war and eventually replaced by an eighteenth-century mansion. In 1164, ten years into his long and eventful reign, Henry II (1154–89) called a council at Clarendon, designed to reassert the king's authority over the legal system following the anarchy of the reign of his predecessor, Stephen (1135–54). Having established that his judges would travel throughout the kingdom to administer a set of common principles of justice (the Common Law), Henry wanted to ensure that his laws, judges and courts would not be challenged by any rival system. And there was a rival system in the form of church courts, administered by the bishops, and applying the laws of the church, known as canon law. The so-called Constitutions of Clarendon laid down the relative roles of the two legal systems and came down firmly on the side of the king's courts. The key provision was the third one, in which clergymen were referred to as clerks. This was not intended as a slight. It was simply a term used to describe those who could read and write, as clergymen could, unlike most of the population (including most royals). It read as follows:

> Clerks cited and accused of any matter shall, when summoned by the king's Justiciar, come into the king's own court to answer there concerning what it shall seem to the king's court should be answered there and in the Church court for what it shall seem should be answered there ... And if the clerk be convicted or shall confess the Church court must not any longer protect him.

The wording is rather clumsy, as is the habit of lawyers, but the meaning is clear. The king's court decides where a case is to be heard and the bishop's court cannot protect clerks (i.e clergy) from the king's justice.

SO WHAT'S THE PROBLEM? CRIMINOUS CLERKS

So what was wrong with that? The problem was that punishments in the bishop's courts were much milder than in the king's courts. As we have seen in Chapter 1, the king's justice could be pretty gruesome, with sentences including mutilation, humiliation and execution. In the bishop's court a serious crime (such as murder or rape) was likely to result in a good ticking off from the bishop, a fine or, at worst, removal from priestly office. Two years before the council at Clarendon, in 1162, Henry had appointed his boon companion Thomas Becket as Archbishop of Canterbury. Becket was born in Cheapside, in the heart of the City of London, to a prosperous but not noble family and showed his keen intelligence and energy during his education at Merton Priory and a London grammar school, probably the one near St Paul's Cathedral. He entered the household of the Archbishop of Canterbury who recommended Becket to the young King Henry as his chancellor, a post that Becket filled to the king's satisfaction. During this time, although he held a number of posts in the church, he was not actually an ordained priest. He was ordained on 2 June 1162 and appointed archbishop the following day, surely a record unlikely to be beaten! Henry was sure that he could count on the support of his friend and former chancellor to bring clergy who committed serious crimes ('criminous clerks' as they were called) within the jurisdiction of the royal courts. He was wrong.

GONE NATIVE

For Becket had gone native. When he was appointed archbishop, Becket, despite his royalist background, became a staunch supporter of the rights of the church, and its priests, to be independent of the king and under the authority of its bishops and, ultimately, the pope. This was an argument that was to persist into the reign of Henry VIII and beyond and, although the problem of 'criminous clerks' was eventually resolved in the king's favour, it took far longer than Henry II anticipated. Becket argued that it was wrong that clergy should be subject to the law of the king in preference to that of the bishop. In particular he argued that, as a representative of God, clergy should not be subjected to physical punishments such as execution or mutilation, 'lest in man the image of God should be deformed'. The most he would concede was that, if a clerk were to commit a serious crime, he would be deprived by the bishop's court of his priestly status so that if he committed any further crimes he could then be punished as a layman. According to a strict interpretation of canon law, Becket had a case, though not all clergy agreed with him, many of them recognising that Henry had a point, as did the lay population who could not understand why clergy should escape heavy punishment for serious crimes. Becket further argued that it would be unjust if a priest were punished by the bishop and further punished by the king. In the archbishop's words ,'God does not judge twice in the same matter.'

'WILL NO ONE RID ME OF THIS TURBULENT PRIEST?' (OR WORDS TO THAT EFFECT)

The argument became increasingly bitter; Henry directed edicts against Becket's supporters and Becket went into exile and threatened to excommunicate his former friend. The Pope, Alexander III, who was thoroughly embarrassed by the dispute between two very headstrong men, eventually brokered a peace settlement, whereby Thomas returned to England in the hope that the two would come to an agreement. However, Henry II had meanwhile arranged for his eldest son Henry to be crowned as his successor and the coronation was performed by the Archbishop of York in Becket's absence. Ultimately the son was to die before the father, but this act enraged Becket. In November 1170, when he returned to England, he suspended the archbishop and other bishops who had participated in the coronation: hardly a diplomatic move. It was this which moved Henry, campaigning in France, to utter the fatal words, 'Will no one rid me of this turbulent priest?' Some dispute the words used and suggest that what he actually said was, 'What miserable drones and traitors have I nourished and promoted in my household, who let their lord be treated with such shameful contempt by a low-born clerk!' The words, whatever they were, would in any case have been uttered in Norman French but the message was clear to four of Henry's knights: Reginald Fitzurse, Hugh de Morville, William de Tracy and Richard le Breton. They set out to confront the archbishop in his cathedral and, when he refused to go to Winchester to answer to the king, they murdered him.

THE CULT OF THOMAS BECKET: 'FRAGRANCE AND VIRTUE'

Within three years of Becket's death, Alexander III declared him a saint. Alexander, despite his earlier reservations about his archbishop's conduct, did not understate the case for sainthood, declaring, 'England is filled with the fragrance and virtue of the miracles which the almighty Lord has wrought through the merits of the holy and venerable man Thomas, former archbishop of Canterbury.' The site of Becket's martyrdom became one of the most important pilgrimage sites in Christendom and Becket shrines were found in Sicily, Spain and in France's magnificent cathedral at Chartres. Henry, whose case for legal reform was drowned in the wave of sentiment which followed Becket's death, made his peace with the Pope and effectively dropped his attempts to bring 'criminous clerks' before the royal courts, except for the offence of high treason. A legend arose in Europe that, as a punishment for the martyrdom of Becket, Englishmen were born with tails, like monkeys, and those who wished to mock the English would walk with their hands behind their backs, covering the area where the tail was supposed to be found.

DON'T MENTION THE SAINT

The veneration of Thomas Becket was to influence the relationship between monarchs and popes for almost four centuries, until Henry VIII broke with Rome over his divorce from Katherine of Aragon. Henry decided to end the embarrassing Becket cult and decreed in 1538 that 'from henceforth the said Thomas Becket shall not be esteemed, named, reputed and called a saint ... and his images and pictures throughout the whole realm shall be plucked down, and avoided out of all churches, chapels, and other places; and that from henceforth the days used to be festival in his name, shall not be observed.' Anyone tactless enough to mention him was to call him 'Bishop Becket'. To make doubly sure, Henry abolished the professorships of canon law at Oxford and Cambridge and replaced them with Regius Professorships of Civil Law – posts which exist to this day. There was to be no more nonsense about church courts rivalling those of the king.

THE USES OF LITERACY

But unforeseen consequences followed. Since literacy was, in Becket's time, almost the exclusive preserve of the clergy ('clerks'), it came to be accepted that anyone who could read could claim 'benefit of clergy' and opt for trial in the bishop's court. In 1351 this loophole was recognised in a statute which extended benefit of clergy to all who could read. Ben Jonson, friend and admirer of William Shakespeare, took advantage of this when charged with manslaughter in 1598, thereby avoiding the hangman.

In time, the test of literacy was debased by requiring the defendant to read the opening verse of Psalm 51: 'Have mercy upon me, O Lord, according to thy loving kindness'. The more intelligent or well-advised criminals therefore took the precaution of learning the verse by heart. The verse became known as 'the neck verse' because it could save a defendant's neck, though in the cases of particularly undeserving criminals, courts could require them to read from a less familiar text.

'UNCLERGYABLE OFFENCES'

By the time of the Tudors, who were never lacking in self-esteem, monarchs had regained their confidence and began to challenge the church courts even before Henry VIII broke with Rome.

Henry VII (1485–1509) decreed that those who could not prove that they were genuinely clergymen could plead benefit of clergy only once and, on being convicted, would be branded on the thumb to prevent them entering such a plea again.

Henry VIII (1509–1547) declared in 1512 that many felonies would be exempt from benefit of clergy, a move condemned by Pope Leo X. This did nothing to help the king when, twenty years later, he was seeking permission for a divorce from Katherine of Aragon.

Elizabeth I's reign (1558–1603) declared many offences 'unclergyable', including murder, rape, sacrilege, burglary, witchcraft and pickpocketing.

King Henry VIII.

Queen Elizabeth I.

CLERGY WOMEN!

In 1624, three and a half centuries before women could be ordained in the Church of England, the benefit of clergy was extended to literate women for theft of goods up to 10*s* (for men the limit was 40*s*); the process had become little more than a device for reasonably well-connected, literate people to escape the more savage penalties for minor crimes, leaving the illiterate masses to suffer the harshest penalties. In 1706 the literacy test was abandoned and benefit of clergy became available to first-time offenders involving thefts of less than 5*s*, though at the same time the death penalty was imposed for thefts of more than 5*s*. More details on this gruesome 'Bloody Code' is in Chapter 7.

CLANDESTINE MARRIAGES
AND A BIGAMOUS PRINCE

Nevertheless, much remained for the bishops' courts to do, though from the late sixteenth century they were mostly concerned with misbehaving clergymen and moral issues, including cases of divorce. Their greatest task, however, lay in dealing with the vexed matter of clandestine marriages: marriages where the banns had not been called in the parish church of the parties concerned. These usually occurred because the partners were marrying without the consent of their families. Impoverished clergy could often be persuaded to perform such ceremonies in return for modest sums of money, the marriages taking place either in churches late at night or in private houses.

The most infamous was the marriage of the prince regent, the future George IV, to the Catholic widow Maria Fitzherbert. With this marriage the prince broke the law twice over: he was not allowed to marry without the permission of his father, the king, under the Royal Marriages Act of 1772, and under the Act of Settlement of 1701, the heir to the throne could not marry a Roman Catholic. He nevertheless married her in 1785, the officiating clergyman having been persuaded to perform the ceremony when the prince offered to pay his debts and thereby secure his release from the Fleet Debtors' Prison. According to some accounts, the marriage took place in the Fleet Prison itself which, as a prison, claimed exemption from the jurisdiction of the church, though others claimed that the ceremony was in Mrs Fitzherbert's Mayfair house. The only penalty that the church courts could impose was to suspend the clergy involved until later statutes which condemned the officiating clergyman to transportation and declared any such marriage to be null and void. In the meantime, the future king's marriage to Caroline of Brunswick, a loveless marriage in 1795 to settle his debts, was bigamous.

EXCOMMUNICATION: BUT NOT PAUPERS

One of the most fearsome penalties available to the church courts was that of excommunication, whereby the offender would be denied access to the communion service and refused Christian burial.

It was a penalty frequently threatened and imposed in the Middle Ages by the Catholic Church and continued to be available to the Church of England after the Reformation and break with Rome. Its object was to bring the offender to his senses and back to the church but it was not imposed, for example, on paupers who were unable to pay their church rates, since they were in no position to purge their offence. In other cases, where excommunication failed to move an offender, the church court could ask the king's court to imprison the culprit in the county gaol until he came to heel. One can only imagine what Thomas Becket would have made of the church's courts depending on the king's courts to enforce their judgements.

FORNICATION, DRUNKENNESS AND MIDWIVES!

By the seventeenth century the bishops' courts were largely concerned with offences against morality rather than crimes. Much of their work involved misbehaving clergymen, though lay people who failed to attend church, fornicated in the churchyard or were guilty of incest also came before the bishop. One of the more curious branches of canon law concerned midwives.

In the sixteenth century the practice arose of midwives being licensed by bishops on the grounds that, since they were present at the birth of babies, they should also baptise them if they seemed weak and in danger of death. In 1567 a midwife called Eleanor Plead was licensed by the Bishop of London, having taken an oath in which she swore not to dismember babies, pull off their heads or substitute one baby for another: an interesting comment, perhaps, upon contemporary practices in childbirth! She also agreed to baptise them in the name of the Father, Son and Holy Ghost. Complaints against midwives could thus be brought before a bishop, whose knowledge of childbirth and obstetric practice was likely to be limited.

In later centuries, this curious arrangement fell into disuse and midwives were subject to no regulation at all, with disastrous consequences for the health of mothers and babies. This was rectified with the passage of the Midwives Act in 1902.

PENALTIES

The penalties imposed by the bishops' courts fell into three categories: excommunication, which has already been explained; humiliation; and, in the case of clergymen, removal from office or defrocking/unfrocking. Humiliation required the offender to appear in the church porch dressed in a white sheet, with bare legs and feet, usually on a Sunday morning. The offence would be recited to the congregation, normally by the offender himself. The culprit would ask for forgiveness and invite the congregation to pray for him. This must have done wonders for church attendance.

Some areas were less merciful than others. In parts of Lancashire, for example, the penitent might be required to stand beside the town crier on market day with a placard round his neck describing the offence. Some offences would not be recognised now. David Jones was a fiery Welshman who, in the 1690s, was in the habit of denouncing the offence of usury (moneylending or banking) and urging his Wiltshire congregation to renounce it. And he was not lacking in confidence, delivering a sermon on the matter from the pulpit of St Mary Woolnoth, opposite the Bank of England in the heart of the City of London in 1692.

By the eighteenth century the church had adopted the practice of commutation whereby offenders, instead of committing an act of penance, could pay a sum of money to the church – a practice which had prompted Luther's sixteenth-century protests against the papacy. Once again, as with those who failed to be brought to heel by excommunication, commuted penalties could be enforced by the king's courts. Poor Becket!

SOME OFFENDERS

Some of the offending clergy were colourful characters. George Jones, a curate of Georgeham in Devon, was accused of drunkenness and found guilty in the bishop's court at Exeter of being a frequenter of alehouses. Indeed, in Exeter, drunkenness was second only to the performance of clandestine marriages in the list of offences, though 'brawling in church' and adultery were also prominent. Exeter was clearly a lively, if risky, place at which to attend church.

In 1675 Philip Havers, a deacon in Essex, was presumably unsure of his ability to pass the examination to become a priest, so he persuaded one William Adams to undergo the examination on his behalf and be ordained and instituted as rector of the country parish of Mount Bowers before Havers took his place. He was found out, deprived of his living and had his orders revoked. He appealed to the Court of Arches, still the appeal court of the Church of England today, which sits in the church of St Mary-le-Bow in Cheapside (home of 'Bow Bells' from the nursery rhyme 'Oranges and Lemons'). He lost his appeal.

So did Dr Edward Drax Free of Sutton in Bedfordshire, who was deprived of his living in 1830 for 'persistent acts of fornication', though only after six years of legal wrangling. Benefit of Clergy had been formally abolished by Parliament in 1827.

'A COSEY, DOSEY, OLD-FASHIONED, TIME-FORGOTTEN, SLEEPY-HEADED LITTLE FAMILY PARTY'

By this time, much of the work of the church courts was being conducted from Doctors' Commons which was, in effect, a cross between an Inn of Court and an ecclesiastical court, based in what is now Queen Victoria Street. Sir Thomas More had been one of its members in the sixteenth century and Charles Dickens, who had been a court reporter, placed his alter ego David Copperfield there for seven years, articled to one of the advocates or proctors. David described his visit to Doctors' Commons with his employer and future father-in-law Mr Spenlow. He wrote of:

> An old gentleman whom, if I had seen him in an aviary, I should certainly have taken him for an owl but who, I learned, was the presiding judge ... Altogether I have never, on any occasion, [seen] such a cosey, dosey, old-fashioned, time-forgotten, sleepy-headed little family party.

Changes in the legal system led to the dissolution of Doctors' Commons in 1865 and the sale of its buildings, which had by then been relocated to Knightrider Street. The buildings and the street were demolished in 1867. The former site of Doctors' Commons is now marked by a plaque on the Faraday Building on the north side of Queen Victoria Street, which became the General Post Office's first telephone exchange in 1902.

THE RECTOR OF STIFFKEY

Harold Davidson (1875–1937) was surely the most notorious of all the clergy who fell before the discipline of the church courts. He came from an ecclesiastical family, numbering twenty-seven clergy amongst his relatives, one of them being an Archbishop of Canterbury. When he left school, he spent a gap year with a group of friends as a professional entertainer before going to Oxford, an early sign of an interest in the theatrical world which was later to contribute to his downfall. The gap year became five years and included an appearance in a professional production of the comedy *Charley's Aunt* before he finally entered Exeter College, Oxford in 1898, having also worked at Toynbee Hall in Whitechapel in the interval.

Toynbee Hall had been set up in 1884 to provide social and educational services to the poor of the East End and continues to do so today. John Profumo worked there for many years after his resignation from the government in 1963, prompted by his affair with Christine Keeler. Davidson also rescued a suicidal teenage girl from drowning in the Thames. These experiences gave Davidson a genuine interest in the welfare of the poor and vulnerable, which further influenced his later controversial behaviour. In 1906, having been ordained and served as a curate at St Martin-in-the-Fields, he was appointed as Rector of Stiffkey (pronounced Stewkey) in Norfolk. He was very popular in his parish, visiting families whether they attended his church or not and, being at this time a man of comfortable means, paying the rents of those unable to afford them, especially at seasons such as Christmas.

During the First World War he served as a Royal Navy Chaplain and when he returned to his parish he found that his wife, a former actress, was pregnant by another man. He forgave her, brought up the child as his own and continued to work in Stiffkey, but would leave his parish on Monday mornings and travel to London to meet young women, claiming that he was concerned with saving them from sinful lives. With his bishop's permission he became chaplain to the Actors' Church Union. In 1925 he was declared bankrupt following some problems not of his own making, in collecting church tithes, and he fell out with one of the local Stiffkey grandees called Hamond who informed the bishop of Norwich, the Rt. Rev. Bertram Pollock, of Davidson's trips to London. Hamond encouraged the bishop to take up the matter in the hope that Davidson would be found guilty of immoral conduct and removed from the parish. Henry Dashwood, solicitor to the Church of England, directed the enquiry but the case faltered when he was informed by the churchwardens that Davidson was the best priest anyone could remember in the parish and that no one, apart from the complainant, would say a word against him.

Undaunted, Dashwood hired a private detective agency, at great expense, to follow the errant rector on his visits to the capital. It transpired that he did indeed approach young women, engage them in conversation, and treat them to refreshments in Lyons tea shops while suggesting that they might have a future on the stage. He was actually banned from some tea shops who thought unseemly the spectacle of a very small (5ft 3in) middle-aged clergyman chatting up nubile young women. Some he invited to Stiffkey for weekend parties, with the agreement of his wife and children. Of the many young women interviewed by the agency only one, Rose Ellis, suggested that he had behaved improperly, claiming that he had tried to have 'connections' with her. This she later retracted, explaining that she had been bribed with port wine by a private detective in a saloon bar and had made the allegations when drunk. Davidson had paid for her to have treatment for syphilis, which she had contracted before he met her. Throughout his ordeal Davidson continued to be supported by many influential figures, notably the Bishop of London (formerly the Bishop of Stepney), who had admired Davidson's work amongst the poor of the East End.

In March 1932 Davidson was brought to trial at Church House, Westminster, before a church disciplinary court on a charge of conduct unbecoming to a clerk in Holy Orders. As the trial unfolded it appeared that, though the rector had a strange obsession with young women often as young as 15, his behaviour was odd and embarrassing rather than immoral. He claimed that his aim was to rescue them from drink and prostitution, his chat-up line often beginning with a claim that he thought that one of his young targets resembled a famous actress, Jean Harlow being a particular favourite. Sometimes he wore a clerical collar and sometimes, when pretending to be a theatrical impresario, he wore a collar and tie. This was not much different from William Gladstone's work amongst fallen women the previous century, though his was without the theatrical undertones. Davidson did succeed in finding jobs and accommodation for some of his young females. The evidence that he had behaved immorally was very thin, apart from a photograph that appeared to show him, in clerical dress, with a 15-year-old girl wearing only a blanket. It seems likely that the picture was a fake, assembled from two quite separate photographs. However by now the press had got its teeth into this *cause célèbre* and during the summer of 1932, hardly a day passed without a new salacious 'revelation' about the rector of Stiffkey.

Judgement was delivered in Norwich Cathedral on Trafalgar Day, 21 October 1932, a day which rather inappropriately marked the triumph of Norfolk's greatest son, Horatio Nelson. As the cathedral echoed to the cries of 'Oyez, Oyez, all persons cited and admonished to appear at this court answer to your names as shall be called', a car screeched to a halt outside in the cathedral close, followed by loud applause. Davidson emerged from the car to the cheers of the crowd and entered the cathedral. He emerged shortly afterwards, now a layman, having been unfrocked, and loudly protesting his innocence. He cried, 'I have been known as the Prostitutes' Padre, the proudest title that a true priest of Christ can hold,' and claimed that if Christ were alive He would be found ministering in Piccadilly.

Davidson spent the remainder of his life doing as he had done in his gap year as a public entertainer, all the while continuing to proclaim his innocence. He spent nine days in a Liverpool prison for an unpaid debt and, on his release, rode through the streets of Blackpool accompanied by two young black women, throwing flowers to the cheering crowds. He was prosecuted for supposedly attempting suicide (then a criminal offence) by threatening to fast to death over his unjust treatment, but was found not guilty and awarded £382 damages against his prosecutors. He met his end in July 1937, at Skegness Amusement Park where he was advertised as 'A Modern Daniel in a Lion's Den'. From the confines of a lion's cage, he was addressing the crowd on the injustices he had suffered. He appears to have tripped accidentally on the lion's tail, provoking the indignant (and normally passive) animal to attack him, with fatal consequences. At the request of his former parishioners he was buried in the churchyard at Stiffkey, his funeral attended by thousands. For many years his grave was well cared for by sympathetic villagers whose community had, through his activities, gained an international celebrity.

Thus ended the career and life of another turbulent priest: not, perhaps, in the same category as Thomas Becket but, in his way, just as well known. Curious visitors rather than pilgrims make their way to Harold Davidson's grave. His demise, in a sense, marked the end of the controversy which Henry II and Thomas Becket began with their dispute. The church courts still go about their business but without such rancour and without attracting the attention of tabloid newspapers or aggrieved knights.

7

THE BLOODY CODE

THE TUDOR CENTURY

William Lambarde's three categories of punishments (infamous, pecuniary and corporal) took on a new significance during the religious troubles of the Tudor reign, when the ever-changing religious views of the kings and queens of the dynasty had the consequence of creating more opportunities for the offence of treason.

Infamous crimes such as treason were punished with hanging, drawing and quartering, these still being inflicted in Lambarde's time on those involved in the Catholic Sir Thomas Babington's plot to replace Queen Elizabeth I with Mary, Queen of Scots. Mary herself underwent the comparatively civilised penalty of beheading, though she was one of many whose decapitation was prolonged because of incompetent axemen.

In 1570 Pope Pius V had unwisely excommunicated Queen Elizabeth I as a heretic, which effectively meant that any Catholic who opposed the queen was not committing a sin, even if it resulted in Elizabeth's death. Elizabeth was not anti-Catholic. She wanted a quiet life on religious matters after the suffering during her sister's reign and stated that she did not seek 'windows into men's souls', but drew the line at attempts to assassinate her. The result of the Pope's

Mary, Queen of Scots, victim not beneficiary of the Babington plot.

act was a series of ill-conceived plots, all of which were discovered by Elizabeth's spymaster Sir Francis Walsingham and the plotters executed. This makes it hard to blame the queen for her suspicion of Catholics and when reports reached her of the hideous suffering of the first of the Babington conspirators to be executed, she ordered that the remaining plotters be executed in a more humane way (though Jesuit priests such as Edmund Campion were not spared).

Lambarde's pecuniary penalties were normally imposed by magistrates for such minor offences as swearing, failing to attend church or playing a musical instrument on the Sabbath. Otherwise loyal Catholics who just refused to attend a Protestant church were subjected to these modest penalties, one of them being the Catholic composer William Byrd (1540–1623), whose music Elizabeth admired.

LEAVE THE BRIDGE ALONE AND STAY AWAY FROM GYPSIES

From the late seventeenth century a series of measures, which collectively became known as the Bloody Code, made a growing number of offences, chiefly against property, subject to the death penalty. In 1688 there were about fifty capital crimes which had been added by Parliament to the Common Law offences of treason, arson, murder, robbery and grand larceny. During the reigns of the first four Georges (1714–1830), further Acts of Parliament produced a tide of capital offences which reflected the contemporary obsession with protecting the rights of property owners who were, of course, very well represented in both Houses of Parliament. By 1830 there were about 300 capital offences, including such bizarre ones as:

Stealing goods worth 5s (25p, not very much even at that time)
Cutting down a tree
Damaging Westminster Bridge
Impersonating a Chelsea Pensioner (possibly with the hope of soliciting money)
Damaging clothes made from imported cloth
Being in the company of gypsies for one month
Strong evidence of malice in a child aged 7–14 years

The most extraordinary of the statutes that created the Bloody Code was the Waltham Black Act of 1723, which was introduced to deal with bands of poachers with blackened faces who were stealing deer from royal forests, a capital offence in Norman times. The first three decades of the nineteenth century were the zenith of the Bloody Code.

The last highwayman to be hanged and buried at the scene of his crime was James Snook (alias Robert Snooks), who suffered this fate near Berkhamsted in Hertfordshire in 1802, his grave still visible in a field grazed by cows close to the A4251. In 1831, George Widgett was the last person to be hanged at Newgate for stealing a sheep, and the following year John Barrett was the last to be executed for stealing from the Royal Mail.

'THE DEATH OF HER CRIME'

In reality, many juries refused to convict defendants for minor crimes which carried the death penalty, and in cases of theft judges would simply declare that the goods stolen were worth less 5s, sentencing

An execution outside Newgate. (*The Newgate Calendar*)

the culprit to a flogging rather than the scaffold. In other cases the sentences were commuted or respited (i.e. indefinitely postponed).

It is estimated that between 1770 and 1830, the last decades of the Bloody Code, 35,000 death sentences were pronounced but only 7,000 were carried out, some 20 per cent of the total. But there were appalling consequences of the Bloody Code.

William Cobbett, never a friend of the judicial system, left an account of a 19-year-old mother of two who had been left destitute when her husband was pressed into the navy and so stole a small quantity of cloth. She was hanged under a law which, in the words of the sentencing judge, was aimed 'Not at her death but at the death of her crime' – in other words, as a deterrent to others.

THE DIVINE WATCHMAKER

The judge's philosophy reflected that of the eminent Anglican divine William Paley (1743–1805). Paley is usually remembered as a campaigner against slavery and for his book, *Paley's Evidences*, which represents God as a watchmaker who created the world as a carefully designed organism, down to the last detail. The book made a deep impression on the young Charles Darwin (1809–82), who later attended Christ's College, Cambridge (as Paley had done) though Darwin's later work overturned that of Paley.

Paley, in his role as criminologist, argued that while there should be a wide range of capital penalties to protect property because 'property being more exposed requires the terror capital punishment to protect it', the penalty should rarely be carried out. He believed that the fear of death alone would be a sufficient deterrent. The argument was weakened by the fact that a large proportion of the crowds who attended executions were themselves habitual criminals. A nineteenth-century governor of Newgate insisted that he had never known a murderer who had not previously attended an execution.

Sir Robert Peel (1788–1850) began to dismantle the Bloody Code when he became Home Secretary in 1822, during which time he also created the Metropolitan Police in 1829. He continued the work after he became Prime Minister in 1834. By the middle of the century the penal code had reverted to the position it had occupied before the seventeenth century, so that once again only treason, murder, robbery and arson in the royal docks remained capital crimes. Juveniles under 16 could no longer be executed after 1908. Even in the nineteenth century, many prominent citizens opposed the death penalty. Having witnessed the same execution in 1840, Charles Dickens and William Thackeray were repelled by the experience, but Dickens held to the view that the deterrent effect of the penalty was probably necessary and, as a rather uncomfortable compromise, concluded that executions should continue, though in private.

1972: NO MORE BEHEADING

Following a number of controversial cases in the 1950s, notably that of Timothy Evans (page 52) and Ruth Ellis (page 125) the movement for the abolition of capital punishment in the United Kingdom gathered pace. The last execution, that of Peter Allen and Gwynne Evans, took place in 1964, following which, in 1965, Parliament voted to suspend the death penalty for five years. In December 1969, Parliament voted to make the abolition of the death penalty for murder permanent, though it remained on the statute book for arson in a naval dockyard until 1971; espionage until 1981; piracy until 1998 and treason until 1998. A working gallows was kept at Wandsworth Prison until 1994, being tested every six months until 1992. Beheading as a method of execution for treason remained on the statute book until 1972.

The effects of the abolition, first of the Bloody Code and later of the death penalty itself, are reflected in the figures below which show the number of executions carried out in England and Wales since 1735:

Dates	Men executed	Women executed	Total
1735–99	6,069	375	6,444
1800–99	3,365	172	3,537
1900–64	748	15	763

The decline in the numbers executed following the nineteenth-century abolition of the Bloody Code is all the more remarkable, given the great increase in the population of England and Wales that occurred between 1801 and 1901, from 9.4 million to 32.5 million.

8

PUBLIC EXECUTIONS AT BARGAIN RATES

THE BELLS OF OLD BAILEY

The most gruesome manifestations of the criminal justice system were the public executions preceded by the 'Tyburn Processions', which took place the day after the condemned sermon. Such was the disorder associated with these processions from Newgate to the place of execution at Tyburn that, from 1763, they were discontinued

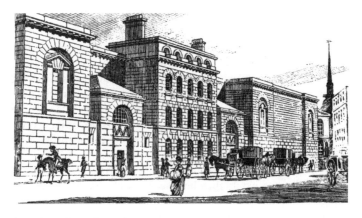

Newgate Prison, about 1820.

and the executions took place, still in public, outside Newgate itself. The ritual associated with the procession began at midnight. A wealthy individual had bequeathed to the City a sum of money which would pay for the great bell of St Sepulchre's church, opposite Newgate, to be rung at midnight by the sexton. This is one of the bells featured in the rhyme 'Oranges and Lemons', which celebrates the bells of the City churches and is mentioned as 'The bells of Old Bailey'. Shortly afterwards a handbell would be rung outside the condemned cell in which those to be executed were spending the night. The ringing of the bell was accompanied by the following verse:

> All you that in the condemned hold do lie,
> Prepare you, for tomorrow you shall die;
> Watch all and pray; the hour is drawing near
> That you before the Almighty must appear.
> Examine well yourselves; in time repent,
> That you may not to eternal flames be sent.
> And when St Sepulchre's bell in the morning tolls,
> The Lord above have mercy on your souls.

Having woken the unfortunate prisoners from any sleep they may have managed to snatch, these words can hardly have cheered them up.

THE TYBURN PROCESSIONS

The following morning, as the bells of St Sepulchre's tolled, the condemned were led into the yard, their chains removed and they were then bound with the rope that would later be used to hang them. More stylish and affluent prisoners would dress especially for the occasion, often in wedding or funeral attire. A white cockade in the hat was variously designed to signify defiance or innocence. Many of them would be drunk with liquor supplied by other prisoners to dull their senses.

The condemned would then be placed in carts for the procession along what is now Holborn, New Oxford Street and Oxford Street to the site of Tyburn, which is marked by a brass plaque set into the ground at Marble Arch. The prisoners were escorted by the Undersheriff of the City and a troop of soldiers, since rescue attempts were not unknown. The hangman, the Newgate Ordinary and the coffins which the prisoners would shortly occupy were also part of the procession. A strict order of precedence was observed:

In the first carts were the highwaymen, the aristocrats of the criminal community who, because they mostly robbed those wealthy enough to ride in carriages or the Royal Mail itself, were regarded with some admiration by the mob who observed the procession.

Lesser criminals followed, sometimes accompanied by their families. A particularly moving sight was recorded of a weeping father trying to comfort his condemned 14-year-old son.

Traitors were last in the procession. Instead of travelling in a cart, they were dragged on hurdles to their gruesome fate.

By the time they left the prison a large, drunken and unruly mob would be lining the streets shouting encouragement or, in the case of unpopular prisoners, insults. There would be a brief stop at St Sepulchre's, where the sexton would exhort the prisoners to 'Repent with lamentable tears, Lord have mercy upon you' following which each prisoner would be handed a beaker of wine and a nosegay to lessen the stench of the crowd and the carts.

Unpopular prisoners would be pelted with missiles, including rotten fruit and dead animals, which would often miss their mark and hit the wrong people, especially when the despatchers of the projectiles were drunk.

Further stops would be made along the route at public houses, notably in an infamous warren of slums known as The Holy Land not far from the present site of Centrepoint and Tottenham Court Road underground station. The last stop for the procession was at the Masons' Arms in Seymour Place. The pub still exists, albeit rebuilt, and at a short distance from its original site since the area has been extensively redeveloped. At each stop the prisoners would be plied with further drink by the excited crowds and on occasion one of the condemned would offer to return the favour 'On the way back'!

GINGERBREAD FOR SALE

At Tyburn itself, the density and excitement of the crowd was such that deaths sometimes arose when onlookers were trampled by those anxious to gain an advantageous view of the spectacle. On at least one occasion the scaffold collapsed and killed a spectator. Such was the disorder that accompanied the execution of Lord Ferrers in 1760 that he took 3 hours to travel from Newgate to Tyburn. Aristocrats were rarely executed in public and Ferrers, a man with a record of violence towards family and servants, had murdered his steward and been convicted following a trial by his peers in the House of Lords.

Tyburn was also a market and a crime scene, since traders like the gingerbread maker Tiddy Doll were regularly present plying their wares and the crowds attracted a multitude of pickpockets.

THE FINAL SPEECH AND MONEY FOR OLD ROPE

Before their executions, the condemned were allowed to make speeches and, since they had nothing more to lose, these speeches were often defiant and critical (and made, of course, very close to the present site of Speakers' Corner at Marble Arch). In 1715, some of those on the losing side in the Old Pretender's rebellion of that year made speeches in favour of the restoration of the exiled Stuarts. Other speeches had less noble motives; the notorious and popular escaper Jack Sheppard, whose exploits are described in Chapter 9, announced from the scaffold that 'he had laid a foundation for raising the reputation of the British thievery to a great height'.

Compassion was not a feature of these occasions, with one female victim, Barbara Spencer, being felled by a stone as she said her final prayers on the scaffold. Nor was dignity much in evidence. A large, fierce Irishwoman called Hannah Dagoe fought with such ferocity at her execution in 1763 that she briefly felled the hangman and then ripped off her clothes, flinging them into the crowd so that the hangman would not profit from their sale. Besides the clothing and other personal effects of his victims, the hangman also profited from the sale of the rope used to hang them – hence the expression 'Money for old rope' – with a premium being paid for rope that was used to execute celebrated or particularly notorious criminals.

Some speeches went on for hours in the hope that a reprieve would arrive. One attempt was made by highwayman Colonel James Turner on 21 January 1663. Samuel Pepys recorded his execution:

> I enquired and found that Turner was not yet hanged. And so I went among them to Leadenhall Street and St Mary Axe, and there I got for a shilling to stand upon the wheel of a cart, in great pain, above an hour, before the execution was done; he delaying the time by long discourses and prayers one another, in hope of a reprieve, but none came and at last was flung off the ladder in his cloak.

MOTHER PROCTOR'S PEWS

Pepys could have witnessed executions in greater comfort at Tyburn, where two female entrepreneurs, 'Mother Proctor' and 'Mammy Douglas', had erected stands from which favoured spectators could watch events unfold in comfort. These pews, as they were called, could hold as many as 10,000 people, some of whom paid as much as £10 for a particularly well-placed seat. Some were virtually season ticket holders with one George Selwyn (1719–91), a Member of Parliament, being a regular attendee. He was often seen to fall asleep during Parliamentary debates but he was an observant connoisseur of executions and corresponded with judges about the best vantage points from which to watch them.

THE TRIPLE TREE

When the speeches were ended the moment of execution arrived. At Tyburn, people were hanged from the 'Triple Tree', a structure which, when viewed from above, was triangular, this shape enabling all three sides to be used for executing twenty-four people simultaneously. The carts in which the prisoners had been taken to Tyburn would draw away, leaving their subjects to suffer slow death by strangulation, a process that could take as long as 30 minutes as the victims gasped helplessly for air while the spectators looked on. In the words of one observer, 'Every contortion of the limbs was hailed with a cheer or a groan according to whether the sufferer was popular or not'. The last stages of their agony were often marked by involuntary emissions of urine, vulgarly described by onlookers as 'Pissing when you can't whistle'. Some had their sufferings curtailed by sympathisers who pulled their legs to break their necks, and occasionally a merciful hangman would perform this office. The development of the 'Newgate Drop', by which a sudden drop broke the neck instantly, ended such indignities.

Some actually survived the hanging. A sailor who became known as 'Half-hanged Smith' was hanged on Christmas Eve 1705 and took so long to die that the crowd demanded that he be cut down. According to his own account:

> After he was cut down and began to come to himself, the blood and spirits forcing themselves into his former channels put him, by a sort of pricking or shooting, to such intolerable pain that he could have wished those hanged who had cut him down.

The Rev. Dr William Dodd was less fortunate in 1777. A successful clergyman, friend to Dr Samuel Johnson and Thomas Gainsborough and chaplain to King George III, he forged a bond in the name of his patron Lord Chesterfield and was sentenced to death. He preached his own condemned sermon in the chapel at Newgate where he was visited by John Wesley, the founder of Methodism, and travelled to Tyburn with a teenage highwayman who was accompanied by his grieving father. Dodd had learned of a method of artificial respiration for those who had been immersed in water, devised by the celebrated surgeon John Hunter. After his execution, his friends removed Dodd's body and, following the Hunter method, immersed his corpse in a warm bath at an undertaker's premises in Tottenham Court Road. The method failed. The corpse remained a corpse.

'EXECUTIONS ARE INTENDED TO DRAW SPECTATORS'

The disorder associated with the executions was so great that in 1783 a decision was taken to move them to Newgate, where they were carried out on a scaffold outside the prison. The abolition of the notorious processions to Tyburn did not please everyone. Dr Samuel Johnson wrote:

> Executions are intended to draw spectators. If they do not draw spectators they don't answer their purpose. The old method was most satisfactory to all parties; the public was gratified by a procession; the criminal was supported by it. Why is all this to be swept away?

Johnson's curiosity was not entirely to be disappointed. The processions ceased but the public was just as eager to watch the executions outside Newgate as they had been on the way to Tyburn, and behaved just as badly.

'DETAILS OF THIS KIND'

One of the tasks of the Newgate Ordinaries was to hear the confessions of the condemned and these became a source of profit as the Ordinaries published vivid, and often highly imaginative, accounts of these confessions to satisfy the macabre curiosity of the reading public. Over 200 such accounts have survived from the eighteenth century and it is estimated that the Ordinaries could make four or five times their annual salary of £35 from these crude and swiftly printed publications, which could be on sale within minutes of the confessor breathing his last. Occasionally the desire for profit overtook the requirements of mercy or justice on the part of the Ordinary.

John Villette, a particularly avaricious Ordinary in the 1770s, accompanied a young boy to Tyburn and learned that, since another person had confessed to the crime, a reprieve was on the way. Presumably alarmed at the prospect of sacrificing sales of the account that he was proposing to publish, he instructed the hangman to proceed since this was no time to worry about 'Details of this kind'. Fortunately, wiser and more merciful counsels prevailed and the boy was spared. Another reprieved man read an account of his confession and death in a newspaper, which had received it from a particularly enterprising and impatient minister.

A mock invitation to the execution of the reviled Jonathan Wilde.

Some criminals were resistant to the pleas of the Ordinaries. When the pirate Captain Kidd was hanged at Execution Dock, Wapping, the traditional site for the execution of pirates, he was drunk by the time he arrived and resisted attempts to confess and repent. The rope that was to hang him broke, at which point his nerve also broke and he repented before he was successfully hanged on the second attempt. His body, like that of other pirates, would then have been left there while three tides washed over it, guarded by a sheriff's officer to ensure that no clothing or other souvenirs were stolen from the corpse. Other criminals refused to confess because they did not want the Ordinary to profit from their confessions, causing one Ordinary to protest, 'Such case hardened rogues as you would ruin the sale of my paper.'

THE EXECUTIONERS

Many executioners had previously followed the trade of butcher, presumably because knowing how bodies were put together meant they were thought to know how to take them apart, especially when beheading was common. They were not always men of exemplary character. A butcher called Rose and his successor, Price, were themselves executed. Another was arrested for debt on his way to Tyburn, thereby earning a reprieve for the three men he was due to execute that day.

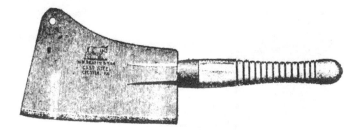

A butcher's cleaver – good practice for executioners.

THE REAL JACK KETCH: 'I CAN'T DO IT'

Two of the executioners' names have come down to us from the seventeenth century. The first is that of Goodman Derrick, who designed a structure to hoist several victims simultaneously, his name having been later applied to the Derrick crane for loading and unloading ships long after his original device was abandoned for more humane methods.

The other is the name of Jack Ketch, whose real name was Richard Jacquet. He was the London executioner between 1663 and 1686, except for a short period when he was himself in prison for insulting a sheriff. He was notably incompetent. In 1683 he took four blows to despatch William Russell for his part in the Rye House plot to kill

A Jack Ketch in the making?

Charles II on his way back to London from the Newmarket races. When the Duke of Monmouth, illegitimate son of Charles II, came to the scaffold two years later for his unsuccessful rebellion against James II, he paid Ketch the generous sum of 6 guineas for a quick end. After multiple blows failed to kill the unfortunate duke, Ketch proclaimed, ''I can't do it,' and attempted to leave the scaffold. He was finally prevailed upon to sever the head with a knife and had to be protected from the angry crowd as he left the scene.

9

THE
ONES THEY
COULDN'T HOLD

SORRY, STEVE MCQUEEN

In the recent past no bank holiday was complete without a screening of *The Great Escape*. This film is closely based upon a true historical event when, in March 1944, seventy-three RAF personnel escaped from the German prisoner-of-war camp Stalag Luft III in what is now Poland. They were led by a Cambridge graduate called Roger Bushell who, along with another forty-nine of the prisoners, was recaptured by the SS and shot on Hitler's orders. His part in the film is played by Richard Attenborough under the name Roger Bartlett. Of the remaining escapees, three made it back to the UK and the other twenty were fortunate to be recaptured by the Luftwaffe and returned to prison. Most of those responsible for the executions were tracked down after the war and were themselves executed. Despite the motorcycling exploits of Steve McQueen, no Americans were involved in the escape. The Americans had camps of their own.

ALFRED GEORGE HINDS

In the 1950s, before televisions were sufficiently widely owned to provide entertainment for bank holidays, a similar service was performed by Alfred George Hinds (1917–91). Having deserted from the British Army during the Second World War, he was convicted for a jewellery robbery in 1953 and sentenced to twelve years' imprisonment. Gaoled in Nottingham Prison, his first escape was through a series of locked doors and over a 20ft-high prison wall, an exploit for which he was given the name Houdini Hinds by the popular press. He spent those eight months of freedom working as a builder and decorator in Ireland, but was tracked down and arrested in 1956.

Hinds was a man of intelligence and instituted a lawsuit against the prison service, alleging that he had been arrested abroad illegally, but this was simply a device to facilitate his next escape attempt. A padlock was smuggled to him by an accomplice while he was in the Law Courts in London's Strand. He was accompanied to the lavatory by two prison guards and when they removed his handcuffs, he pushed them into the cubicle and used the padlock to secure the door. He fled into the Strand but was recaptured attempting to leave the country. This did not spare the blushes of the unfortunate prison guards who were greeted, as they returned to the prison, by exultant prisoners chanting:

> Oh, dear, what can the matter be
> Two screws got locked in the lavatory

Hinds escaped a third time, this time from Chelmsford Prison, and dealt in used cars before being arrested for a motoring offence under the name William Herbert Bishop. His true identity quickly became evident.

After this, his final escape, Hinds devoted his time to a study of the English legal system as it applied to imprisonment, arguing that since his escapes had been through unlocked doors (owing to slackness in prison regimes), he had not committed an offence by taking advantage of those weaknesses. He made his way through the entire legal system, finishing with a personal appearance before the House of Lords in 1960 where he spoke for 3 hours. His appeal finally dismissed, he served a further six years at Parkhurst Prison on the Isle of Wight. In 1964, while still in Parkhurst, he brought a libel action against former Chief Superintendent Herbert Sparks of

New Scotland Yard's Flying Squad for some articles that Sparks had written about Hinds in a Sunday newspaper. Hinds was awarded damages of almost £800.

He later sold his life story to the *News of the World* for a reported five-figure sum and in 1966, following his release from prison, he published his own account of his encounters with the legal and prison systems, entitled *Contempt of Court*. He was also much in demand as a speaker and during a debate at the Regent Street Polytechnic (now the University of Westminster), he was kidnapped by students as a stunt but repeated his earlier escape at the law courts by locking them in the basement room that they had intended for him. Hinds, a man described as being 'of high intelligence and low cunning' became a member of Mensa, a society for those with high IQs, and retired to the Channel Islands where he died in 1991.

JACK SHEPPARD

The British prison system has had many embarrassing escapes, but surely no escapee has been as persistent and successful as Jack Sheppard (1702–24) who in his short life managed to escape from Newgate Prison on three separate occasions. Sheppard was born in Spitalfields and originally followed his honest father into the trade of carpenter, but by 1723 he and his brother had become partners in a flourishing criminal business in burglary and what would now be called shoplifting. One of their fellow criminals, known as 'Edgeworth Bess', specialised in 'fencing' (disposing of stolen property) and the two, passing themselves off as man and wife, were committed to Newgate to await trial in 1723. With the aid of a file smuggled in by a visitor, Sheppard removed their fetters and a bar from their cell window. They descended to the yard via a rope made of knotted sheets and scaled the great external wall, using the locks and bolts of the gate as footholds, before disappearing into the criminal community of St Giles, close to the present site of Tottenham Court Road underground station.

Foolishly, instead of fleeing from where he would be recognised, he continued to execute his trade in London and even rented a

Jack Sheppard finally meets his end.

stable in Horseferry Road to store his ill-gotten gains. He was recaptured in August 1724, sent to Newgate and sentenced to hang. His escape on the second occasion was surprisingly easy, consisting of opening a hatch in the prison and fleeing to Spitalfields, where he proceeded to dispense advice to admiring fellow criminals on the finer points of larceny and escapology. A few days after his escape, he stole three watches from a watchmaker in Fleet Street and took the precaution of retiring to Finchley.

After a few days at large he was identified (possibly for a reward), arrested and returned to Newgate where the authorities took the precaution of handcuffing him and securing his leg irons to a staple in the floor of his cell. Such was his notoriety by this time that his gaolers were able to charge unheard-of sums to visitors for the opportunity to see the infamous Jack Sheppard thus confined. His final escape required ingenuity of a high order. With the aid of a nail, he removed the handcuffs and the padlock that attached his leg irons to the staple in the cell floor. Still in leg irons, he began to climb the chimney in his cell until he found his passage barred by an iron rod. He scraped out the mortar which held the rod in place and climbed into a room above his cell. Using the iron rod as a crowbar, he wrenched off the room's locked door and passed through further doors by similar means, using the crowbar to open the final door by wrenching off its hinges. Sheppard had now reached the top of a high wall, from which he could only drop to freedom by breaking every bone in his body, so he returned to his cell via the route he had taken and collected a sufficient number of blankets to make a rope, by which he descended to the garret of a neighbouring house, where he fell asleep.

He spent the next few days in Soho, listening to ballads about his escape until, betrayed by a barman, he was arrested and returned to Newgate a fourth time, earning his gaolers even more fees from curious visitors. His celebrity status was now such that, while held in the condemned cell, he was visited and painted by Sir James Thornhill, sergeant painter to King George I. He was also the subject of many cartoons celebrating his exploits. Nevertheless he was hanged at Tyburn on 16 November 1724 before an unusually sympathetic crowd. The authorities took the precaution of searching him before he left Newgate and found a sharp knife in his pocket with which he was planning to cut himself loose from the ropes that bound him and flee into the welcoming crowd. His death was followed by a violent struggle between his many admirers and some of his friends who were suspected of being beadles of the College of Surgeons; it was feared they wanted his young, healthy corpse for dissection. He was eventually buried in the churchyard of St Martin-in-the-Fields, now just off Trafalgar Square, the churchyard having been lost in succeeding centuries.

GEORGE BLAKE

George Blake (birth name George Behar) was born in 1922 in Rotterdam to a Dutch mother and Egyptian-Jewish father who had become a British subject. He was educated at the English School in Cairo, where he came under the influence of his Communist cousin, Henri Curiel, a creed which shaped the rest of Blake's life. During the Second World War, Blake worked for the anti-Nazi Dutch resistance and escaped to Britain where he joined the Secret Intelligence Service, MI6, eventually being sent to Seoul in South Korea. In June 1950, Blake was captured by the North Korean forces during the early stages of the Korean War and was 'turned' by them into a dedicated Communist. At the end of the war he was released and returned to Britain, where he was sent to work in Berlin, then on the front line of the Cold War. In Berlin he made contact with the KGB and proceeded to destroy the Western intelligence network in Berlin and Eastern Europe, sending many agents to their deaths until he was himself identified by a defecting Soviet agent in 1961. He was sentenced to forty-two years in prison and sent to Wormwood Scrubs.

On 22 October 1966 he escaped with the help of two anti-nuclear campaigners and made his way to Moscow, where he would have found a community of spies well established after their escape from justice. The first of the 'Cambridge Spies', Guy Burgess and Donald Maclean, had fled in 1951 after learning that they were about to be exposed. Guy Burgess, always a sad exile, had died in 1963 after a lifetime of abusing alcohol, though Maclean lived on until 1983.

Kim Philby, the third member of the group, died in 1988 while the other two of the ring – whom the KGB called 'The Magnificent Five' – escaped conviction, Anthony Blunt being exposed as a spy in 1979 and John Cairncross in 1990. Blake is often bracketed with the 'Cambridge Spies', though he did not attend Cambridge University and seems to have had little contact with them in Moscow. He always denied being a traitor on the grounds that he had never felt British: 'To betray you first have to belong. I never belonged.' He continues to live in Moscow and in 2007, on his eighty-fifth birthday, he received the Order of Friendship from Vladimir Putin.

LIFE ON THE RUN: RONNIE BIGGS AND THE GREAT TRAIN ROBBERY

The year 2013 marked the sixtieth anniversary of the crime which brought Ronnie Biggs notoriety: the Great Train Robbery of August 1963, when the Glasgow–London Royal Mail train was halted close to Bridego Railway Bridge near Mentmore on the West Coast main line and robbed of £2.6 million (the equivalent of almost £50 million in 2013). The robbery, involving about fifteen people, was well planned but the robbers' hideout, Leatherslade Farm near Brill in Buckinghamshire, was quickly discovered. The hideout was, in the words of the police at the time, 'One big clue' yielding sufficient evidence in the form of fingerprints to convict nine of the robbers.

Exemplary sentences were handed down with Ronnie Biggs, whose part in the robbery was relatively minor, receiving thirty years. After fifteen months Biggs escaped from Wandsworth Prison with the aid of a rope ladder and a waiting furniture van and made his way to Brussels and then Paris. Over the next several years, with the police always in pursuit, Biggs, sometimes accompanied by his family, made his way to Adelaide, Melbourne, Panama and Brazil. Shortly after his arrival in Brazil, Biggs's son Nicholas, aged 10 and still in Australia, was killed in a car crash. Biggs was tracked down by a *Daily Express* reporter in Rio de Janeiro and the newspaper was swiftly followed by Scotland Yard's Jack Slipper, whose attempt to extradite Biggs was frustrated by the fact that Biggs's girlfriend was pregnant with his child, meaning that the expectant father was entitled to remain in Brazil. An attempt by a group of ex-soldiers to kidnap Biggs and claim a reward failed when their boat broke down off Barbados, which had no extradition treaty with Britain.

By this time, the proceeds of the robbery had long gone and Biggs was reduced to entertaining visitors at barbecues in return for payment, regaling them with fanciful accounts of his very minor role in the robbery. One of his visitors (who probably got in without payment) was the footballer Stanley Matthews.

In 2001 Biggs returned voluntarily to Britain, the return orchestrated by his Brazilian son Michael, who reportedly received a payment of £20,000 from *The Sun* (which also paid for a private jet). It appears that the main reason for his return was nostalgia, including, in his own words, a wish to 'walk into a Margate pub as an Englishman and buy a pint of bitter'. This did not prevent Biggs from beginning an immediate campaign to secure his release from Belmarsh Prison on compassionate grounds related to his health, but successive Home Secretaries resisted his pleas, with Labour's Jack Straw commenting that Biggs was 'wholly unrepentant'. He was finally released on compassionate grounds in August 2009, shortly before his eightieth birthday, and attended the funeral of his fellow Great Train Robber, Bruce Reynolds, in March 2013. He died in December 2013.

10

THE VILLAINS

Some of those who have unwillingly entered the system of justice have had few redeeming features.

THE THIEF-TAKER

A humiliating end awaited Jack Sheppard's nemesis and contemporary Jonathan Wild (1689–1725), whose life ended in Tyburn the year after Sheppard.

Born in Wolverhampton, Wild went to London in about 1712 (having abandoned his wife and child) and soon established himself in the city's criminal underworld by offering to 'recover' stolen property for its owners. Having learned of the theft of a valuable item, Wild would approach the victim and offer to find the stolen item in return for a commission. In this way he would extract from the grateful owner something approaching the full value of the property, whereas the thief using a 'fence' would earn only a fraction of the sum. This left a hefty commission for Wild, who was not associated with the crime itself. He even advertised his services in the *Daily Courant* in May 1714 from his office in what is now the Barbican:

Lost on 19 March last, out of a Compting House in Durham Court, a Day Book of no use to anyone but the owner ... Whoever will bring them to Mr Jonathan Wild over against Cripplegate Church shall have a Guinea Reward and no Questions asked.

He soon became more ambitious and began to organise robberies, while being sure not to become directly involved himself, using the robbers, in effect, as salaried employees. And finally, when business was poor, he boosted his income by turning in some of his robbers to the authorities for rewards, in this capacity describing himself as Thief-taker General. On one occasion the Lord Chief Justice issued him

Jonathan Wilde: thief, 'fence' and supergrass.

with a writ for the arrest of two highwaymen. In effect Jonathan Wild was poacher and gamekeeper at the same time. His annual income has been estimated as £25,000, an unimaginably large sum at the time.

He made a fatal error when he helped to secure the arrest of the popular hero Jack Sheppard though; the crowd outside the Old Bailey cheered when another criminal, called 'Blueskin Blake', attempted to slit Wild's throat. In February 1725, following a falling-out with

Jack Sheppard in Newgate.

some of his fellow criminals, he was arrested and charged with 'procuring false evidence to swear persons into facts they were not guilty of'. He defended himself by drawing attention to seventy-five criminals who had been hanged or transported on the basis of his evidence (much of it no doubt fabricated) and offered the names of more criminals to George I in return for a reprieve. This craven attempt to save his own skin by betraying others was unsuccessful and his execution, on 24 May 1725, was a scene of public rejoicing. After brief interment in St Pancras, his body was obtained by the Royal College of Surgeons, in whose museum it remains in Lincoln's Inn Fields.

His activities were celebrated in John Gay's *Beggar's Opera* in 1728 only three years after his death and, 200 years later, in Bertold Brecht's *Threepenny Opera*, based on Gay's work and first produced in 1928.

THE ACID BATH MURDERER

John George Haigh (1909–49) had a very strict upbringing by parents who were members of the austere Plymouth Brethren sect. Haigh became a gifted pianist and choirboy at Wakefield Cathedral in his native Yorkshire. After a brief career in commerce, he married but was shortly afterwards gaoled for fraud, his wife leaving him and giving up their baby girl for adoption while he was in prison. He was also disowned by his family. A short period as chauffeur to William McSwan, the owner of amusement parlours, was followed by further sentences for fraud which gave him time in prison to contemplate the perfect murder: dissolve the body of the victim in acid to destroy the evidence.

He was released from gaol and his first victim was McSwan. Haigh killed him in a basement in Gloucester Road, Kensington and later murdered McSwan's parents. In each case, he placed the bodies in drums of sulphuric acid and poured the resultant mixture down a manhole.

He cashed their pension cheques, sold their properties and moved into the Onslow Court Hotel in Kensington. He later moved to Crawley, where he rented a small workshop and installed his acid and drums.

Here, when he ran short of money, he murdered and disposed of a married couple called Henderson and a final victim, a fellow resident at the Onslow Court Hotel called Olive Durand-Deacon. There were also three other victims to whose murders Haigh later confessed.

When the police were notified of Mrs Durand-Deacon's disappearance, they investigated the other residents of the Onslow Court Hotel and learned of Haigh's record as a fraudster. When they searched his workshop in Crawley, they discovered papers and other evidence referring to his victims, and an examination of the contents of the drums revealed some human gallstones and part of a denture which was identified as Mrs Durand-Deacon's by her dentist.

The trial at Lewes Assizes featured the Attorney-General, Sir Hartley Shawcross, for the prosecution and a future Lord Chancellor, Sir David Maxwell-Fyfe, for the defence. Both had served at the then-recent Nuremberg Trials of Nazi war criminals. Haigh pleaded insanity, but the jury swiftly found him guilty. He was hanged by Albert Pierrepoint at Wandsworth Prison in August 1949.

There was another conviction at the trial. The editor of the *Daily Mirror*, Silvester Bolam, was gaoled for referring to Haigh as a murderer before the jury gave its verdict.

JAMES HANRATTY AND THE A6 MURDER

In August 1961 a scientist called Michael Gregsten was enjoying a tryst with his mistress, Valerie Storie, in a field at Dorney Reach near Eton in Buckinghamshire, close to the scene of Britain's later rowing triumphs in the Olympic Games of 2012. Their activities were interrupted by the arrival of a gunman, who ordered them to drive in a number of directions before telling them to stop at Deadman's Hill, on the A6 near Clophill in Bedfordshire, a few miles south of Bedford. There the abductor, described by his surviving victim as having a cockney accent, shot Michael Gregsten dead before raping and repeatedly shooting Valerie Storie, also leaving her for dead. In fact she survived and, though paralysed from her injuries, played a major part in the events that followed.

Two prime suspects were identified in a case which attracted the attention of the press to a degree which was almost equal to that of Jack the Ripper in the previous century.

The first was a man called Peter Alphon who, until his death in 2009, encouraged journalists in search of a story to fill their pages with the idea that he was the A6 killer. In 1967 he actually called a press conference to announce that he was the culprit; though his 'confessions' were equivocal and later withdrawn, it was hard to escape the conclusion that he was a lonely inadequate who welcomed publicity. His moment of fame owed much to the fact that he had stayed in a cheap hotel in north London, the Hotel Vienna, where some spent cartridges had been found. The hotel had also been used in the period following the murder by the second suspect.

James Hanratty was a small-time criminal whose parents had successfully resisted attempts by his local authority in Burnt Oak, North London, to have him sent to a special needs school, although he was illiterate when he left school in 1951, aged 15. He worked for a time as a refuse sorter for Wembley Borough Council but suffered a serious head injury in a cycling accident which left him unconscious for 10 hours. This, and a subsequent incident which led to spells in Sussex hospitals, may have affected his mental capacity. After this he embarked on a career as a petty criminal, housebreaker and car thief, which led to a spell in Wormwood Scrubs and an attempt at suicide. Attempts by his despairing father to employ him as a window cleaner led only to further crimes and spells in prisons in Maidstone, Strangeways (Manchester) and Durham.

On 24 August, two days after the murder, the murder weapon, a revolver, was found under the back seat of a London bus. The weapon was later linked to the cartridge cases found in the Hotel Vienna and the hotel manager, who himself had a criminal background, first identified Peter Alphon as the occupant of the room where the cartridges were found. Alphon was eliminated from the investigation after Valerie Storie failed to recognise him at an identity parade, and the hotel manager then stated that Hanratty (calling himself James Ryan) had occupied the room. Valerie Storie picked him out at an identity parade, partly due to his distinctive cockney accent.

There was little evidence in the days before DNA other than Valerie Storie's identification and the fact that Hanratty changed his alibi during the trial. He had no record of violence and no apparent motive for the murder. The jury at Bedford Assizes found Hanratty guilty and, after a failed appeal, he was hanged at Bedford Prison on 4 April 1962, still protesting his innocence. He was 25 years old and one of the last people to be hanged for murder.

THE A6 DEFENCE COMMITTEE

Hanratty became more famous after his execution than he ever was during his short and troubled life. A group called the A6 Defence Committee, headed by *Private Eye* journalist Paul Foot, set about unearthing evidence and alibis (Hanratty had claimed to be in Liverpool and then, partway thought the trial, at Rhyl in North Wales on the fatal day) to prove his innocence. None of these persuaded the authorities that Hanratty had been wrongly convicted, though many observers had their doubts.

Eventually the development of more sophisticated DNA techniques enabled a sample of DNA to be obtained from a handkerchief in which the murder weapon had been wrapped, and from semen in Valerie Storie's underwear. These proved to closely match members of Hanratty's family. In 2001 Hanratty's body, which had been buried rather than cremated, was exhumed and the match between his DNA and that found on the handkerchief and underwear was, in the words of the judges who heard the appeal in 2002, 'certain proof of guilt'. So what led James Hanratty, a housebreaker and car thief, to commit murder and rape? A friend of the author, who was in Hanratty's class at school, remembers him as a rascal, but with no malice or violence in his nature. One suggestion is that Michael Gregsten made a sudden movement which Hanratty thought threatening and, alarmed, discharged the gun by accident. Thereafter panic took over, leading to further desperate acts of violence.

Paul Foot, who died in 2004 two years after the final appeal, went to his grave convinced that Hanratty was innocent.

DR HAROLD SHIPMAN

It is likely that the most prolific serial killer in British history was a much-respected family doctor in Hyde, Greater Manchester: Dr Harold Shipman. After qualifying as a doctor in Leeds, Shipman worked as a GP in Todmorden, Yorkshire, where he was fined for forging prescriptions of pethidine for his own use, attended a drug rehabilitation course and then became a GP in Hyde, Greater Manchester in 1977. He was revered by many of his patients, not least for making unscheduled visits to enquire about their health, during some of which visits he administered medication which, he assured them, they needed.

Suspicions were aroused about the number of death certificates he was signing, but they were allayed until he signed the death certificate of Kathleen Grundy, a former Lady Mayor of Hyde, who had previously been in good health. Shortly before her death she had apparently changed her will, excluding her family and leaving all her estate to Shipman. Mrs Grundy's daughter questioned this and a police investigation revealed that the will had been made on Shipman's typewriter. Exhumation of the bodies of some of his patients revealed that he had frequently administered lethal doses of diamorphine shortly before their deaths and that he had falsified medical records on his computer. In 2000, a jury found him guilty of murdering fifteen of his patients, though a subsequent enquiry suggested that he may have killed as many as 250 people, of whom 80 per cent were women.

Sentenced to life imprisonment, Shipman committed suicide in Wakefield Prison in 2004 at the age of 57.

11

THE FRAUDSTERS

Fraudsters are by no means a novel feature of the criminal justice system and two in particular played a major part in the construction of the London Underground. Indeed, without them much of it might never have been built.

DOWN THE TUBES

The London Underground Railway first entered service in 1863, running from Paddington to Farringdon in the City of London. The opening of this first line, the Metropolitan Railway, was delayed by about five years because much of the money set aside by the Great Northern Railway (GNR) to invest in the new line was embezzled by one of its employees. The GNR wanted to see the line built so that its passengers would have a swift journey from its terminus at King's Cross to their destinations in the City but, when the money was called upon by the promoters of the line, the GNR learned that £170,000 of it had been appropriated by one of its servants, Leopold Redpath. Much of this huge sum was being spent on entertaining aristocratic friends at his magnificent houses at Weybridge and in Regent's Park: all supposedly on a clerk's salary of £500 a year. Eventually unmasked, Redpath was one of the last convicts to be sentenced to transportation to Australia for life, where he became a popular and companionable resident, according to one of his descendants who made contact with the author. Even with this setback, the Metropolitan Railway was a success from its first days in January 1863, despite being drawn by steam locomotives for the first forty years of its life, which filled its tunnels with steam and smoke.

DEATH IN THE LAW COURTS

Redpath was not alone in his tendencies. In 1897 an English millionaire called Whitaker Wright (1845–1904) financed the construction of what was to become the Bakerloo Line, linking Waterloo, London's busiest passenger station, with Baker Street, the apex of the Metropolitan. Wright had made a fortune from mining in the USA and invested £700,000 in the new line, on which construction began in 1898.

As costs mounted, Wright ran into difficulties and attempted to unload shares in the line on to other shareholders while talking up their value and those of his mining companies, in a series of optimistic but misleading statements. Wright fled to France and from there to the USA, where he was arrested and brought back to London to

Coal mining: the source of Whitaker Wright's fortune, soon to be lost on the Bakerloo Line.

face a charge of larceny. On 26 January 1904 he was convicted of defrauding investors in his companies to the tune of £5 million. Mr Justice Bingham sentenced him to 'the severest punishment which the Act permits ... penal servitude for seven years'. Wright left the courtroom protesting his innocence and announcing his intention to appeal. He then collapsed, dead from a cyanide capsule he had swallowed. More alarmingly, when his clothes were searched, the police found a loaded revolver which he had been carrying throughout the trial.

Following his death, further details emerged concerning his lifestyle. He owned a fine estate at Witley in Surrey, the facilities of which included a billiard room, encased in glass and submerged in a lake in the grounds. It's still there and may be viewed on the web by entering 'Witley Park Billiards Room' in a search engine.

DEATH IN A GOLD BEDSTEAD

Almost exactly two years later, on 29 December 1905, an equally flamboyant benefactor of the London Underground died in his extravagant home in New York's Fifth Avenue, lying in his gold bedstead which had once belonged to the King of Belgium. This was Charles Tyson Yerkes, who had been gaoled in Philadelphia for financial fraud and drummed out of Chicago, where he had brought disaster on a number of investors in his City transit schemes. So he came to London, where he raised £12 million to purchase and electrify the District Railway (now the District Line); complete the Bakerloo Line which had been left unfinished by Whitaker Wright; and begin the construction of the Piccadilly Line and the northern section of the Northern Line from Charing Cross to Hampstead via Euston. He raised the money by making extravagant claims about the profits that the electrified railways would be sure to make, though it is worth noting that the financiers of the City of London were always suspicious of Yerkes, who raised much of the money on the continent and in the USA. The City was wiser in those days!

Following the death of Yerkes, an examination of his company's finances showed that his railways were on the verge of bankruptcy. From this they were rescued by a German-Jewish philanthropist called Edgar Speyer. Yerkes had left his fine art collection to the citizens of New York, but his American affairs were as disorderly as those of his London Underground railways and his creditors seized the pictures (and presumably the gold bedstead) before the citizens of New York had a chance to view their legacy. Upon such men as Yerkes did we depend for the construction of the London Underground Railway. By comparison with these predecessors, Boris Johnson, who is now responsible for the network, is a shrinking violet!

ALBERT GRANT

The Underground was not the only feature of London to receive the attention of fraudsters. In 1873, a financier called Albert Grant (1830–99) offered to pay for the refurbishment of Leicester Square, which was at that time an embarrassing dump in the heart of London's West End. In the centre of the square was a vandalised statue of George I, while on the northern side of the square was a heap of rubble which had been created by a gas explosion. There were also a few sad remnants of Leicester House, the seventeenth-century home of the Earls of Leicester, which gave the square its name and had been demolished in 1806. Finally, there were a few bankrupt businesses and some decaying advertising hoardings. Albert Grant bought out the owners of the square and paid for it to be landscaped and ornamented with statues of four former residents of the square and its vicinity: Isaac Newton, Joshua Reynolds, William Hogarth and the surgeon John Hunter. In the centre of the square, in keeping with the theatrical area in which it is located, is a statue of Shakespeare on a plinth on which is also recorded a tribute to Albert Grant.

There is, however, no reference to the fact that Albert Grant was a noted fraudster. Born in Dublin as Abraham Gottheimer, he changed his name to Grant in 1863 and made his fortune as a 'company promoter'. An early practitioner of the black art of direct mailing, he invited clergymen, widows and other small investors to buy shares in such enterprises as the Labuan Coal Company and the Emma Silver mine. If these existed, which is doubtful, they made money only for Albert Grant, who raised £24 million by such means, of which £20 million was never seen again.

A brief spell as MP for Kidderminster was interrupted when he was found to have bribed voters. In 1873 he built a huge house near Kensington Palace which he used once, for a 'Bachelors Ball', before it was seized by creditors, demolished and the main staircase sold to Madame Tussauds. After being made a hereditary baron of the new kingdom of Italy for developing a shopping centre in Milan, he insisted on being addressed as Baron Grant. He died in poverty in 1899, his obituary notice recalling, 'Many an ancient adventure of his as company promoter, mine owner, millionaire and bankrupt'. His memorial is Leicester Square which he paid for, albeit with money extracted from his fellow citizens.

HORATIO BOTTOMLEY

Horatio Bottomley (1860–1933) was born in Bethnal Green and brought up in an orphanage. He learned something of legal processes when he joined a firm of legal shorthand writers, and made use of this experience in 1885 when he appeared in the bankruptcy courts. Like Albert Grant, he was skilled at persuading his fellow citizens to invest in his projects and, like Grant, he created one enduring legacy when he founded the *Financial Times* to promote his money-making schemes. He also mirrored Grant in that he was elected to Parliament as MP for Hackney South in 1906 and 1910, though in 1912 he lost the seat when he was declared bankrupt.

In 1906 he founded the patriotic magazine *John Bull*, which survived until the 1960s, and used it to attack Germany and all things German during the First World War, arguing that Germany 'must be wiped off the map of Europe' and its colonies confiscated. He also embarked on a tour of Britain in which he used his undoubted skills as an orator to promote recruitment to the armed forces, often receiving a fee for doing so. In 1918 he returned to

Parliament, once again as MP for Hackney, and promoted the John Bull Victory Bond Club, a forerunner of the Premium Bonds, with prizes rather than interest payments.

Careful work by a detective who later became a founder member of the Flying Squad demonstrated that the John Bull Victory Bond Club was a fraud which had helped to restore Bottomley's shaky finances. He was sentenced, like Whitaker Wright, to seven years in prison. When the chaplain of Wormwood Scrubs observed him in the traditional convict occupation of sewing mail bags, he enquired: 'Sewing, Bottomley?' 'No, reaping,' came the reply. Bottomley was released from prison in 1927 and performed in music halls until his death in 1933.

12

THE VICTIMS
OF INJUSTICE

JUSTICE MISCARRIES: 'LET HIM HAVE IT'

Justice doesn't always get it right and two executions from the 1950s stain its conscience. The first was that of Derek Bentley (1933–53), a petty criminal whose early years are reminiscent of those of James Hanratty. During the Second World War, Bentley suffered head injuries when the house in which he was living was bombed. He was later found to have an IQ of between 66 and 77 (the average being 100) which, in the harsh words of the time, categorised him as 'borderline feeble-minded'. Like Hanratty, he worked for a time in the waste disposal business of his local authority, Croydon. In February 1952 he was rejected for military service on the grounds that he was 'mentally substandard'.

By November 1952, he had also served three years at an approved school for theft when he and his 16-year-old friend Christopher Craig attempted to burgle the warehouse of a confectionery company in Croydon. Craig supplied Bentley with a knife and knuckleduster while Craig himself carried a revolver. The two thieves climbed on to the roof of the warehouse.

Alerted by a neighbour, the police arrived and, after a struggle, arrested Bentley while Craig remained on the roof armed with his pistol. Police witnesses maintained that, while in police custody, Bentley shouted, 'Let him have it, Chris,' as a police officer climbed on to the roof to apprehend Craig. Bentley had warned the police that Craig was armed. Doubts remain about whether Bentley uttered the fatal words, 'Let him have it,' and further doubts about what he meant if he did use them. Did he mean 'Let him have the gun', knowing that there was no hope of escape in the presence, by then, of several police officers? Or did he mean, as the prosecution maintained, 'Shoot him'? The first policeman to reach the roof was PC Sidney Miles who was shot dead. Having emptied the gun, Craig jumped from the roof, injuring himself.

Charged with murder, at the trial Bentley argued that he was under arrest at the time PC Miles was shot. Much was made of the words, 'Let him have it,' allegedly used by Bentley, though denied by him and Craig. The defence also argued, unsuccessfully, that Bentley's low intelligence made him unfit to stand trial. The jury took 75 minutes to find both guilty. Craig, aged 16, who had fired the shots, was too young to hang and served ten years in prison. The jury recommended clemency for Bentley but the Home Secretary David Maxwell Fyfe disagreed and Bentley was hanged, aged 19, on 28 January 1953.

In 1991, a film on the case was released under the title *Let Him Have It* and after a long campaign by his family, Derek Bentley's conviction for murder was quashed by the Court of Appeal, a decision welcomed by Craig who, after release from prison in 1963, led a blameless life as a plumber.

JUSTICE MISCARRIES: CULPRIT OR VICTIM?

Ruth Ellis (1926–55) was born Ruth Hornby in Rhyl on the North Wales coast, her father a cellist and her mother a Belgian refugee. The father later changed his name to Neilson. In 1941, at the height of the Blitz, the family moved to London where Ruth, while working as a waitress, became pregnant by a Canadian soldier and gave birth to a son known as Andy who went to live with Ruth's mother. Following work as a nightclub hostess and prostitute, she married a divorced dentist called Ellis, a jealous alcoholic, and bore him a daughter whom he refused to acknowledge as his own. Ruth eventually returned to live with her parents.

At this point Ruth's chaotic life appeared to take a turn for the better when she became the manager of the Carroll Club, which attracted a number of what would today be called celebrities, including the future world motor racing champion Mike Hawthorn and another racing driver called David Blakely. Ruth moved in with Blakely, but neither was faithful to the other and Ruth became the mistress of a well-to-do businessman called Desmond Cussen, moving into his comfortable flat north of Oxford Street while continuing to feud with Blakely, who had caused her to have a miscarriage when he punched her in the stomach.

On 10 April 1955, she pursued Blakely to the Magdala Club in Hampstead, greeting him as he left. Blakely ignored Ruth, whereupon she drew a revolver and shot him dead with several rounds. She asked a bystander to call the police, was taken to Hampstead police station and confessed to the crime. She was asked only one question by the prosecuting barrister, Christmas Humphreys, QC: 'When you fired the revolver at close range into the body of David Blakely, what did you intend to do?' She replied, 'It's obvious. When I shot him I intended to kill him', but also admitted, 'I shall die still loving him.'

This guaranteed a guilty verdict, which the jury reached in 14 minutes. In 1955 it also guaranteed a death sentence which was duly pronounced by the trial judge, Mr Justice Havers, grandfather of the actor Nigel Havers. However, the judge wrote to the Home Secretary Gwilym Lloyd George (from an even more famous family) recommending a reprieve as it was a *crime passionel*, but the recommendation was rejected. Ruth declined to appeal the sentence, but on the day before her execution she told her solicitor that the gun used in the crime had been given to her by Desmond Cussen, a fact not disclosed to the jury. A final appeal was made by the solicitor to the Home Office, without result. In a final letter from prison to Blakely's parents she wrote, 'I have always loved your son and I shall die still loving him'. The execution was carried out by Albert Pierrepoint on 13 July 1955 at Holloway Prison. Anthony Eden, the Prime Minister at the time, left the matter to the Home Secretary but was believed to have felt uncomfortable about the case.

The case was extremely controversial at a time when opposition to the death penalty, though fragile, was growing in strength. Ruth Ellis was seen as a woman who had been exploited by men, even to the extent of suffering a miscarriage at Blakely's hands, and as much victim as culprit. Raymond Chandler wrote to the *Evening Standard* denouncing the 'medieval savagery' of the sentence and *Daily Mirror* columnist 'Cassandra' (William Connor), not known for his liberal views, wrote that 'The one thing that brings stature and dignity to mankind and raises us above the beasts will have been denied her – pity and the hope of ultimate redemption'.

The consequences for Ruth's family continued long after her death. In 1958 her husband, George Ellis, hanged himself and in 1969 Ruth's mother, Berta Neilson, was found unconscious in a gas-filled room and never fully recovered. In 1982 Ruth's son Andy, aged 37, killed himself. Sir Cecil Havers, the judge at Ruth's trial, had made annual contributions to his upkeep and Christmas Humphreys, the prosecuting lawyer, paid for his funeral. In the 1970s, Holloway Prison underwent extensive rebuilding and Ruth Ellis's body was exhumed and reburied in the churchyard of St Mary's, Amersham, with a headstone inscribed 'Ruth Hornby, 1926–1955'. Her son destroyed the headstone shortly before taking his own life.

Ruth Ellis was the last woman to be executed in Britain and the case was one of the strongest influences on the course of events which led to the abolition of capital punishment. The last execution took place in 1964 when Peter Allen and Gwynne Evans were executed for murdering a van driver called John West in the course of theft.

ROGER CASEMENT: TRAITOR OR PATRIOT?

Roger Casement (1864–1916) was born near Dublin to a Protestant father and Catholic mother who had her son rebaptised as a Catholic when he was 3 years old. After his father's death when he was 13, the teenager was brought up by Protestant relatives in Ulster, an ambiguity which was later reflected in his troubled relationship with the British Empire of which he was a citizen and servant. In 1880 he joined the Elder Dempster shipping line based in Liverpool and in 1901 he was appointed British consul in the Congo, then mostly administered by King Leopold of Belgium, for whom it was virtually a personal possession. Casement, of his own initiative, produced a detailed report describing the appalling human rights abuses perpetrated in the king's name and with his connivance in his quest for rubber and other natural resources in which the territory was rich. The conditions in which the native Congolese were obliged to work amounted to slavery and Casement's report had such a sensational impact that the British Parliament demanded a revision of the agreements made at the Berlin Conference of 1884–5, under which Leopold held the territory. This duly followed and the Belgian Parliament took over responsibility for the land, administering it as the Belgian Congo.

In 1906 Casement, now a hero, was sent to South America where he revealed similar abuses of Peruvian Indians by the British registered Peruvian Amazon company; men and women were confined to stocks and starved and flogged, many of them dying as their children looked on. Some of the culprits were arrested by the Peruvian authorities while others fled, leading to an improvement in conditions for the native Peruvians.

In 1913 Casement retired from the consular service, having been knighted for his work in the Congo and Peru, and became involved in fundraising for the Irish independence movement. At the outbreak of war in 1914 he sought to enlist the support of the German government for the Irish cause, suggesting that an uprising in Ireland using German money and guns would divert British troops from the Western Front. The attempt by Berlin to send armaments to Ireland was known to the British, however, who intercepted the ship carrying them. Casement travelled to Ireland to warn the Irish leaders that their rising was doomed, but Casement was arrested shortly after landing near Tralee in April 1916, three days before the Easter Rising in Dublin which, while spectacular, failed in its purpose and led to the execution of many Irish nationalists.

Casement was imprisoned in the Tower of London and prosecuted for treason, though the Treason Act of 1351 applied only to activities on British soil, whereas Casement's discussions had taken place in Germany. On a loose interpretation of the Act, Casement was found guilty of treason and hanged at Pentonville on 3 August 1916, attended by a Catholic priest, despite pleas for clemency from such figures as Sir Arthur Conan Doyle and George Bernard Shaw. Strangely Joseph Conrad, whose novel *Heart of Darkness* had referred to many of the Congolese atrocities which Casement exposed, was unsympathetic to Casement's cause. He was regarded by the Irish as a martyr and the priest who attended his execution claimed that Casement was a saint: 'We should be praying to him instead of for him'.

Following his death, an attempt was made to undermine his character by the release of the Black Diaries which showed Casement to be a homosexual at a time when homosexual practices were illegal; many remembered the fate of Oscar Wilde, whose disgrace had occurred twenty years earlier. Doubts existed at the time about the authenticity of the diaries, though subsequent research has suggested that they are genuine.

In 1965 Casement's body was removed from the Pentonville Prison Cemetery and sent to Dublin, where he was given a state funeral with full military honours. Half a million people filed past his coffin before his burial in Glasvenin Cemetery, Dublin. He was stripped of his knighthood before his death, though the British cabinet minutes of the decision to repatriate his remains to Ireland refer to him as Sir Roger Casement. He remains an Irish hero, with many buildings and monuments in Ireland named after him, and his burial site in Dublin is a place of pilgrimage.

THE NOT THE GREAT TRAIN ROBBER

One of the greatest cases of injustice in the twentieth century concerned William (Bill) Boal, who was sentenced to twenty-four years in prison (later reduced to fourteen years) for the Great Train Robbery of August 1963, in which he was not involved. The first of the robbers to be arrested was Roger Cordrey, who had been the robbers' electrical expert and wired the signal which stopped the train at Sears Crossing near Cheddington, Buckinghamshire. Bill Boal was a friend of Cordrey and, in return for some earlier favours, Boal helped Cordrey to find a rented flat above a florist's shop in Bournemouth, far from the scene of the crime. The two men also rented a garage for Cordrey's car and aroused the suspicions of the landlady when they paid three months' rent in advance, paying in used 10s notes. The publicity surrounding the robbery ensured that anyone found to be in possession of large quantities of cash fell under suspicion. It didn't help that the landlady was a policeman's widow.

The police found £141,000 in Cordrey's car (almost half the total sum that was recovered out of the £2.6 million stolen) and charged Boal with receiving stolen goods. The other robbers all knew that Boal had not been involved in the robbery and some of them later said they felt bad about his sentence. But none of them did anything about it at the time. Boal died in prison in 1970, a bitter man, the victim of injustice and of abandonment by those who could have helped him.

MONSTER OR FLOWER MAKER: THE STRANGE CASE OF THE NEWGATE MONSTER

Perhaps the strangest case of injustice is that of the Newgate Monster, who may not even have existed. In the 1790s the gaolers at Newgate had a celebrity prisoner to rival Jack Sheppard and were able to charge visitors extravagant sums for the right to see him.

It all started in May 1788 when Maria Smyth, the wife of a doctor, complained that she had been indecently propositioned by a man while she was walking in Fleet Street. Similar reports followed from other women and the man, variously described as tall or short, stocky or thin, gentlemanly or vulgar in appearance, became more active. His *modus operandi* included the practice of sticking a sharp object into his victim, usually in the bottom, though occasionally the thigh was preferred. Soon the culprit was celebrated in a play called *The Monster*, which attracted large audiences to the spectacle of seeing young actresses with their bottoms evidently pierced by the monster's fiendish contraptions. The celebrated cartoonist James Gillray drew a carton entitled 'The Monster Disappointed of his Afternoon Luncheon', which showed the monster contemplating in dismay a young woman's bottom covered by a protective shield.

Monster or flower maker?

Eventually one of the early victims, Anne Porter, identified a man called Rhynwick Williams as the man who had assailed her hind parts, having seen him in the street. A search of his modest lodgings revealed no incriminating evidence and in the trial which followed, one victim placed Williams in London on a day when a witness claimed he had seen him in Weymouth, 130 miles distant. Since the witness was a Bow Street Runner this might have been thought convincing evidence. Williams was employed as an artificial flower maker and his employer testified that Williams had been at work when many of the attacks supposedly took place, as did many of his colleagues.

Nevertheless, the magistrates found Williams guilty of damaging garments under a statute of 1721, designed to discourage unemployed weavers from protesting against the import of cheap cloth from India. A scapegoat was needed to appease public anxiety and Williams was unfortunately the only available candidate. After further legal arguments before a primitive appeal tribunal called The Twelve Judges of England (the Court of Appeal came into existence only in 1907), Williams was sentenced to six years in Newgate where his notoriety earned him the gratitude and admiration of his gaolers, who profited from his presence and allowed him to live in comfort. He resumed his trade of making artificial flowers, which were sold at a premium to reflect his celebrity status. While in Newgate he married, had a son who was baptised at nearby St Sepulchre's church in 1795 and was released in 1796, after which he disappeared from history.

WITCHCRAFT

One group of people who were victims of injustice were witches, and no examination of the penal codes in England is complete without some reference to its approach to witchcraft. This owes much to King James I (1603–25). In 1589, while returning from Denmark with his bride, the future Queen Anne, a storm arose which, for reasons best known to himself, he attributed to witchcraft. The Tudors had been reasonably relaxed about witches, their statutes demanding the death penalty for witches only when harm had been caused, though benefit of clergy was specifically denied for such offences. The Witchcraft Act of 1604, following James's accession to the English throne, prescribed the death penalty for anyone who 'invoked evil spirits' and was used heavily by Matthew Hopkins, the self-appointed Witchfinder General. James himself had written a book on the subject called *Daemonologie*, which argued that where there was one witch there must be more.

THE WITCHES OF PENDLE

It was in the middle of James's reign that England's most infamous witchcraft trials occurred – the 1612 trials of the Pendle Witches. It all began when a young woman from the Pendle area of Lancashire called Alizon Device asked a passing pedlar from Halifax, John Law, for some pins. Pins were used for treating warts but also for love divination (identifying a potential husband) and Law declined to give them to Alizon, either because she was begging or because it was not worth unpacking his wares for such a small transaction. A few minutes later Law stumbled and fell, either because he lost his footing or, possibly, because he suffered a mild stroke. Either way, the story gained currency that Alizon had brought this misfortune upon Law by witchcraft and she reportedly visited him later and sought his forgiveness.

BEWITCHING A HORSE

There followed a series of 'confessions', beginning with Alizon's own, and allegations which gradually drew in more people from the Pendle area and a few from Yorkshire. Much of the impetus of the enquiry which followed was due to rural Lancashire being regarded as a rather lawless place, inhabited by many recusant Catholic families whose loyalty to the Stuarts was questioned. There is even a suggestion that William Shakespeare spent some time during his lost years in the previous century as tutor to a Catholic family. The judges who heard the trials in 1612 were both anxious to curry favour with the king. One, Sir James Altham, had mishandled a case in York, which had led him to fear for his future as a judge. The second judge, Sir Edward Bromley, was hoping for promotion and knew of James's interest in, and fear of, witchcraft.

Given James's belief that witches hunted in packs, it is hardly surprising that twelve people from the Pendle area were identified as witches, of whom eleven went to trial – nine women and two men. They included a mother and daughter: Anne Whittle and her daughter Anne Redfern. The charges varied, from murder by witchcraft and bewitching a horse to causing the River Ribble to overflow its banks. Six of the witches came from two families, each family accusing the other and each family with a background in healing by what we would now call natural cures – easily represented as magic at the time. One of the principal witnesses was a 9-year-old child who claimed that her mother, Elizabeth Device, was a witch with a familiar in the form of a brown dog called Ball, who helped out with some of her murders. Elizabeth's son James said that he had seen his mother make a clay figure of one of her victims. That was about as good as the evidence got. One of the eleven was found not guilty and the other ten were hanged after trials at York and Lancaster Assizes, much of the evidence being in the form of confessions.

It has been estimated that from the fifteenth to the eighteenth century, fewer than 500 people were executed for witchcraft in England, so the Pendle witches deserve their notoriety on the grounds of numbers alone. In Scotland on the other hand, King James's place of birth, there were 450 witchcraft trials during his reign alone. Clearly witches preferred to stay north of

Hadrian's Wall. The judges did well from the trials. Bromley gained the promotion he sought and Altham's career continued to flourish until his death in 1617. Pendle has subsequently revelled in its unusual claim to fame and celebrated the 400th anniversary of the tragedy in 2012 with a festival and exhibition.

THE BELVOIR WITCHES

Two years after the Pendle trials, in 1619, two sisters called Margaret and Philippa Flower were hanged at Lincoln. They had worked at Belvoir (pronounced 'beaver') Castle, the home of the Earl of Rutland, and had been dismissed for pilfering. Soon afterwards the earl's young heir, Henry, died and the sisters were accused of killing him by witchcraft. The usual paucity of evidence was accompanied by tales of pacts with the devil and the sisters' association with demons in the form of familiars, these being animals like cats. Pet ownership could be a hazardous business in the reign of James I.

Suspicion later settled on King James's favourite George Villiers, Duke of Buckingham, who married the earl's daughter Katherine and hoped to inherit the earl's estates in the absence of a male heir. By promoting the witchcraft nonsense, Villiers not only diverted attention from himself but further ingratiated himself with his witch-obsessed sovereign. He didn't profit from his marriage for long. He remained a favourite with James's son, Charles I, but was unpopular with almost everyone else and was assassinated in 1628 in a Portsmouth pub.

THE D-DAY WITCH

By 1735, the Witchcraft Act of that year reflected an increasingly sceptical attitude towards the subject of witches, appropriate in the century which witnessed the Enlightenment. Few now believed in witchcraft, so the Act imposed penalties on those who pretended to be able to summon spirits, foretell the future or otherwise obtain money on false pretences.

Oddly, the last person to be prosecuted under this Act was Helen Duncan who, in 1944, claimed to commune with the spirit of a sailor who had died on the battleship HMS *Barham* in 1941, the loss of which had not been revealed to the public. It seems that some superstitious intelligence officers feared that she would reveal the plans for the D-Day invasion of Normandy, so she was arrested during a séance, charged with contravening the Witchcraft Act and gaoled for nine months, by which time Normandy was securely in Allied hands.

13

THE ONES
WHO GOT AWAY
WITH IT

A SPOT OF RICHARD
AND A CHILD MURDERER

Richard III ruled for barely two years (1483–5), one of the shortest reigns in English history, yet he is one of our best-known monarchs. His name has even entered prison slang; 'Richard' is used as an expression in cockney rhyming slang to mean a prison sentence. When a criminal says that he is due for a spot of Richard, then Richard refers to Richard the Third, which rhymes with bird, a term for a spell in prison. And the last of the Yorkist kings had the unparalleled misfortune of having his character assassinated in one of Shakespeare's most memorable plays, a character further sharpened by one of Sir Laurence Olivier's most vivid performances.

There is a further connection with Richard and crime in the unlikely shape of the headquarters of the Post Office at St Martin's Le Grand. Founded as a monastery and college in the reign of Edward the Confessor (1042–66), it became a place in which criminals could seek sanctuary. According to Sir Thomas More, Miles Forrest, one of those accused of the murder of the Princes in the Tower, sought sanctuary in St Martin's and, in More's words, 'rotted away piecemeal' there. The murder was never solved.

THE EASTBOURNE DOCTOR

At the time of Dr Harold Shipman's trial, many recalled that of Dr John Bodkin Adams, a general practitioner in Eastbourne, where more than 150 of his patients died in mysterious circumstances, of whom 132 left him items in their wills. After moving to Eastbourne, where he lived with his mother and cousin, Adams fell into the habit of inviting himself to patients' homes for meals and helping himself, uninvited, to mementoes of patients who had died. He lived in style in a large house and received his first 'inheritance' from a patient in 1935. By 1956, he was a wealthy man with famous patients including Lord David 'Chariots of Fire' Burleigh and the Duke of Devonshire.

In 1956, Eastbourne police received a report of a suspicious death and proceeded to investigate in the face of an uncooperative British Medical Association, which advised other local doctors to observe 'professional secrecy' when dealing with the police. In fact, two Eastbourne doctors did co-operate with the investigation. Adams was evasive when questioned by police about drugs records, legacies and other aspects of his practice, but was eventually charged with murder. Some evidence went missing, other evidence was kept from the jury and not revealed until many years later and Adams himself did not give evidence in his defence, his defence barrister later confessing that Adams would have been a disastrous witness: 'greedy, pig-headed, loquacious and dishonest'.

Adams was found not guilty and retired to a lunch of lamb chops, boiled potatoes and greens, followed by a large bowl of jelly. He died in Eastbourne, a wealthy man, in 1983. His biographers have sometimes been less kind to him than the jury was.

'THE ULSTERMAN'

There are strong reasons for believing that one of the principal actors in the Great Train Robbery of 1963 is still at large, having escaped the best efforts of the Metropolitan Police and the Post Office Investigations Unit to find evidence that would convict him. It has been suggested that he worked for the Post Office, informed the gang of the quantities of money to be found on the train and was the only one of the conspirators to receive his full share of the loot (about £150,000) and escape justice altogether. Only two members of the gang ever met him, these being Buster Edwards, who hanged himself in 1994 and Gordon Goody, who is still alive and has announced that he will name him, an Ulsterman.

A RIPPING VICTORIAN MYSTERY

We end our tale of criminals who escaped justice with the most notorious of all: Jack the Ripper. Between August and November 1888, five women were murdered in Whitechapel, a poor part of East London: Mary Ann Nichols, Annie Chapman, Elizabeth Stride, Catherine Eddowes and Mary Jane Kelly. These are known as the 'canonical five' murders, since they occurred in a short period and

Frances Cole was the last murder attributed by the press to the Ripper, though this may have been due more to press excitement (in this case *The Illustrated Police News*) than to evidence.

FINDING the MUTILATED BODY IN MITRE SQARE .

The Ripper strikes again: the fourth victim, Catherine Eddowes, is discovered in Mitre Square, Whitechapel. (*The Illustrated Police News*)

in a small area of Whitechapel, and were characterised by extreme violence towards the victims, which involved severe knife wounds and, in some cases, disembowelling.

Other murders in the same area at about the same time are possibly attributable to this most infamous serial killer, who appears to have been influenced by a belief that the women were prostitutes. The last of these possible Ripper murders was that of Frances Coles, which occurred in February 1891. The murders attracted unprecedented coverage in the press and were a source of great embarrassment to the Metropolitan Police. Over 2,000 people were interviewed, over 300 were investigated and 80 were detained, but no one was ever convicted. Despite this failure, the murders ceased and it was assumed that the killer had died, left the country or been imprisoned for other offences. The absence of a culprit did not prevent newspapers reporters, writers, police and amateur sleuths from suggesting a number of candidates, some plausible, some improbable and some truly exotic. Indeed the task of identifying the Ripper has attracted more charlatans in search of fame and money than the Loch Ness monster or alien invaders.

A ROYAL RIPPER?

Prince Albert Victor was perhaps the most exotic suspect of all. The grandson of Queen Victoria, Prince Albert Victor, Duke of Clarence, was the eldest son of the Prince of Wales (later Edward VII) and therefore second in line for succession to the throne. The theories that this rather dim royal was the Ripper appear to have owed much to a desire by its proponents to gain notoriety and promote the sales of their books and articles. They involve a supposed secret marriage by Albert to a shop assistant (particularly shocking because she was a Catholic); a love child; syphilis; and a conspiracy involving Queen Victoria and her prime minister to liquidate anyone who knew of Albert's unusual marital arrangements. Surprisingly, the Loch Ness monster did not make an appearance. There was a problem with the theory though: an examination of the Court Circular reveals that Albert was dining with the queen when he should have been roaming the streets of Whitechapel, knife in hand.

Walter Sickert, an artist, was also suspected and this theory actually featured in some literary works, but the story is spoilt by the fact that the artist appears to have been in France while some of the murders were taking place. But why let the facts get in the way of a good story?

'Jill the Ripper' was suggested by Arthur Conan Doyle who, besides his vicarious crime-solving activities in the person of Sherlock Holmes, occasionally ventured into the real world of crime. He proposed a woman, possibly posing as a midwife so she could move about with blood on her clothing without attracting suspicion and who would be trusted by the female victims.

Charles Dodgson, better known as Lewis Carroll, the author of *Alice's Adventures in Wonderland* and *Through the Looking Glass*, a quiet, innocuous clergyman, was perhaps an even less plausible suspect. The theory is based upon supposed cryptic references in Carroll's works and is as plausible as the theory that William Shakespeare's works were written by Francis Bacon. To date, no one has accused William Shakespeare of being the Ripper, but watch this space.

John Pizer, a Polish Jew who worked as a bootmaker in Whitechapel and was known as 'Leather Apron' for the bootmaker's leather apron that he wore, was named by a newspaper as the Ripper after he was arrested by Police Sergeant William Thicke on suspicion of murder in September 1888 at the height of the Ripper frenzy. Bootmakers were familiar with knives and other cutting instruments, which were the mark of the Ripper's butchery. Pizer was able to call another police officer to testify that he had been engaged in conversation with Pizer while watching a fire in the London Docks at the time that one of the murders was committed: the perfect alibi. Pizer recovered libel damages from at least one newspaper.

Francis Tumblety, a quack doctor, was implicated in the death of one of his patients in the USA and was arrested for complicity in the assassination of Abraham Lincoln, but in each case he escaped prosecution. In November 1888, at the time of the final Ripper murder, he was arrested for suspected homosexual activity, whereupon he skipped bail and fled to the US. His behaviour was connected in the press to the Ripper enquiries, which were at their height. Anyone arrested for being drunk would probably have attracted the attention of some sections of the press but

No one escaped suspicion; note the Holmes and Watson figures in the background. *(Illustrated Police News)*

homosexuals, even in the years before Oscar Wilde's disgrace, would have been considered capable of anything. The New York City Police Chief declared that 'there is no proof of his complicity in the Whitechapel murders', and Tumblety lived out a thenceforth blameless life in the USA.

Aaron Kosminski was also suspected. In his memoirs, the Assistant Commissioner of the Metropolitan Police at the time of the Ripper murders, Sir Robert Anderson, wrote that a Polish Jew had been identified as the Ripper but that the only reliable witness was also Jewish and would not testify against a fellow Jew. Kosminski, one of many Polish Jews living in the East End at the time, was identified as the Ripper by two of the investigating officers, one of them writing his name in the margin of Anderson's memoir. In 1891 Kosminski was admitted to Colney Hatch lunatic asylum, at about the time that the last of the more doubtful Ripper murders occurred. His insanity consisted of hallucinations and a fear of being given food by others, but his behaviour in the asylum showed no violent tendencies. He died in 1919.

David Cohen, another Polish Jew, was later identified as an alias for Nathan Kaminsky, a Whitechapel bootmaker who, like his countryman John Pizer, would have worn a leather apron for his trade and would have been familiar with knives. The name David Cohen was often applied to Jews whose real names were hard to pronounce for their gentile neighbours. Kaminsky was treated for syphilis, which might have given him a grudge against prostitutes, and disappeared from records in mid-1888, the same time that 'David Cohen' appeared on the scene. He was incarcerated at Colney Hatch asylum at the time the murders ended and showed violent tendencies there before his death in 1889. It has been suggested that the disappearing Kaminsky was confused with Aaron Kosminski (see previous entry), a fellow inmate of Colney Hatch who thus fell under unwarranted suspicion.

James Kelly murdered his wife in 1883 by stabbing her, and was sent to the Broadmoor asylum for the criminally insane. He escaped shortly before the first Ripper murder in 1888 and vanished, possibly to the US, where he appears to have worked as an upholsterer, an occupation that would have required him to become skilled in the use of knives. A New York policeman called Norris argued that Kelly moved around the US, leaving behind him a trail of Ripper-like murders in each city that he visited. In 1927, to the surprise of all, Kelly turned himself in to the Broadmoor authorities and died there of natural causes two years later.

James Maybrick was a Liverpool cotton merchant whose wife Florence was convicted of poisoning him with arsenic in a controversial trial in 1889. His candidacy for the role of Jack the Ripper was based upon a diary in which he confessed to the murders and which was published by a man called Barrett in the 1990s. Examination of the diary revealed a number of factual errors in the 'confessions', handwriting which bore no resemblance to that of Maybrick himself and ink of a kind that was not available until the 1970s. Nice try, though.

Other candidates have included an assortment of wife murderers, fraudsters, poisoners, policemen, abortionists, journalists, fantasists, lunatics, a Russian secret policeman and associate of Rasputin and two royal physicians. The evidence against them ranges from the highly implausible to the non-existent. Indeed, there is considerable doubt about whether some of the Ripper suspects ever lived at all.

14

THE INVASION OF THE BODY SNATCHERS

NOT ENOUGH EXECUTIONS

Although the exhumation of bodies from graves is usually associated with criminal investigations, as in the case of Dr Harold Shipman (see page 117), it was occasionally done by royal command for reasons of state. In 1278, Edward I ordered the opening of a tomb at Glastonbury which reputedly contained the remains of King Arthur and Queen Guinevere, and Edward attended their reburial before the high altar of Glastonbury Abbey. The site is now marked by a notice, since the abbey was dissolved and the tomb destroyed on the orders of Henry VIII.

The decline in executions following the dismantling of the Bloody Code (see Chapter 7 and the statistics referring to executions on page 90) was good news for petty criminals but bad news for one group of people who needed a steady flow of corpses: the (later Royal) College of Surgeons, particularly the anatomy schools. The Murder Act of 1752 specified that the College of Surgeons was entitled to ten cadavers of executed criminals each year, to be used for purposes of dissection and teaching, this being an alternative to the former practice of hanging the bodies in gibbets at crossroads to deter others. The hospitals of St Thomas's and St Bartholomew's had similar entitlements. Further specimens were available from the hangman in

Body snatchers at work.

return for payment: the accounts of the College of Surgeons for the eighteenth century include payments of 2*s* 6*d* (12.5p) to the Newgate hangman and further payments to the college's beadles for injuries sustained in collecting cadavers from Tyburn.

AN UNUSUAL CURE FOR WARTS

This could be a hazardous task. Friends or relatives of the hanged usually regarded dissection as an indignity and would often put up stout resistance to the beadles who were attempting to secure the cadaver. Reference has already been made to the determination with which Jack

Sheppard's corpse and that of the Rev. Dr William Dodd were spirited away by supporters. Unsurprisingly, in the case of a really unpopular victim like Jonathan Wild, the beadles had an easier task.

Another criminal the crowd were glad to see despatched to Surgeons' Hall in 1767 was Elizabeth Brownrigg who, despite occupying the normally merciful profession of midwife, so maltreated a servant girl who had been sent to her by the Foundling Hospital that the child died of her injuries. Even in such cases, retrieving the cadaver was not without its hazards. Hanging by strangulation,

Elizabeth Brownrigg, midwife, killed through maltreatment a servant girl sent to her by the Foundling Hospital. (*Newgate Calendar*)

which prevailed before the 'Newgate Drop' brought about a swift death, caused the body to perspire. It was widely believed that this 'death sweat' was a cure for warts. This meant the cutting down of the body would often be followed by a stampede by onlookers wishing to rid themselves of these unsightly features.

And the beadles' efforts were not always rewarded as expected. In November 1740, the beadles triumphantly delivered to the college the body of a robber called William Duell, who 'came round' on the dissecting table, to the great consternation of the surgeons.

Elizabeth Brownrigg awaits execution.

'RESURRECTION MEN'

In the nineteenth century, as medical science progressed and the number of cadavers legitimately available from the hangman began to fall, there arose a trade in disinterred corpses, the practitioners of this dark art being known as 'resurrection men'. In the eighteenth and early nineteenth century, Scotland, particularly Edinburgh, prospered as schools of anatomy and medicine were set up. The young Charles Darwin was amongst those sent there by their parents in the hope that they would become successful doctors. Darwin was not a promising pupil, fleeing from an operating theatre because he could not face the spectacle of surgery before anaesthetics (though he flourished in a later career).

In Edinburgh in the seventeenth century, one hanged corpse was divided into ten parts for dissection by students at the anatomy school and, in 1728, students there had a similar experience to their London fellows with 'Half-Hanged Smith' (see page 96), when the cadaver of Maggie Dickson came back to life before their eyes.

'PRAYING HOWARD':
'BODIES ARE PROCURED IN
LONDON ALMOST EVERY DAY'

Some of the resurrection men showed considerable enterprise in their pursuit of bodies. One, called 'Praying Howard', was an assiduous attendee of funerals in order to learn where bodies were buried in fresh earth, easily dug up to reveal a fresh corpse. He would also note the position of the coffin in the ground so that the resurrection men could excavate the grave above the head. This made it easier to remove it from the coffin by grasping it round the shoulders, after which the earth could be replaced together with any flowers or decorative shells, leaving the empty grave apparently undisturbed to the casual observer. Howard may have been one of those who supplied cadavers to the needy Scots, provoking a complaint from the London surgeons to their Edinburgh colleagues: 'Bodies are procured in London almost every day. We leave anyone to form their own opinion whether it would not be an easier affair at Aberdeen.'

But the resurrection men, despite their insensitivity, did not have an easy task. An eminent Scottish surgeon called Robert Liston (1794–1847), who had his own reservations about the activities of the resurrection men, on one occasion frightened off two teams of bodysnatchers by hiding behind a tombstone dressed entirely in black and leaping out as they began their work, causing them to flee.

More conventional ways of protecting freshly buried corpses were adopted by relatives of the deceased. Some cemeteries near medical schools posted nightwatchmen in towers, while others invested in a kind of cage called a mortsafe, which would be padlocked across a fresh grave for about six weeks after which, it was calculated, the body would have decomposed to a point where it was no longer of value to the grave robbers.

DICK TURPIN RIDES AGAIN

The body of the highwayman Dick Turpin was removed despite being buried in a deep grave, in secret, at night. The bodysnatchers were apprehended by angry citizens and Turpin reburied in the graveyard of St George's, Fishergate, where it is marked by a gravestone bearing the highwayman's name. The church itself no longer exists, but the site is opposite the Roman Catholic church of St George's.

BURKE AND HARE: HOW TO RECOVER THE RENT

There was a particularly active trade in Edinburgh because of the work of a very popular teacher of anatomy called Robert Knox. By 1828 Knox had 500 students, which required a larger supply of corpses for dissection than were likely to be obtained by legitimate means. Many of the cadavers that were delivered to him were supplied by two Irish immigrants called William Burke and William Hare, whose names have become synonymous with the resurrection trade.

Medical students – but no bodies on which to practise.

They seem to have entered the business by chance when one of Hare's lodgers died of natural causes, owing him back rent. Hare recovered the arrears, and more, by selling the cadaver to Knox for £4. Encouraged by this venture, Burke and Hare, with the assistance of Burke's mistress, Helen McDougal, and Hare's wife, Margaret Laird, started to lure drunks and other homeless people to their home with the promise of lodgings. They killed them by suffocating them, a method that left no marks. In summer a corpse fetched £8, a tidy sum when labourers were lucky to earn 4s (20p) for a day's work. In winter the price rose to £10 because

Burke and Hare prepare for their night's work.

the frozen ground was harder and it was therefore more difficult to disinter buried corpses (although they were also better preserved in the cold). Since Burke and Hare produced their own corpses and did not have to rely on burials, such matters did not concern them.

However, they became careless. In November 1828, the corpse of Madge Docherty was discovered at Burke's flat by a fellow lodger. Alarmed (especially since he could have been the next victim), the lodger informed the authorities, who arrested Burke. Hare denied all knowledge of the matter and actually gave evidence against his business partner, having been offered immunity if he turned King's evidence. For this Hare was reviled by the Edinburgh public.

William Burke's execution, amidst much rejoicing.

The trial took place on Christmas Eve 1828 and lasted for 24 hours. When Burke was found guilty on Christmas morning of the murder of Mary Docherty (other suspected murders being left on the file), the judge expressed regret that, for such an atrocious crime, he could not order Burke's body exhibited in chains as had been the custom in earlier centuries. Instead he ordered that his body 'should be publicly dissected and anatomised' and further expressed the hope that Burke's skeleton be preserved as a record for posterity. The execution was attended by 20,000 people, some paying 5s for an advantageous view. The judge's wish was granted, as Burke's skeleton was placed on display at the University of Edinburgh anatomy museum.

Hare fled to England, pursued by angry mobs wherever he was recognised, and disappeared from history, though one report suggests he was pushed into a lime pit, blinded and ended his days as a beggar on the streets of London. Knox, the surgeon who had provided a ready market for the pair's merchandise, was not prosecuted. Public opinion found him guilty by association, however, and his house was stoned and he was hanged and burned in effigy. He fled to London and worked as an anatomist at Brompton Hospital until his death in 1862. He was celebrated in rhyme, along with his suppliers:

Burke's the butcher, Hare's the thief,
Knox the boy that buys the beef.

Sir Walter Scott did not think the behaviour of the Edinburgh crowds was much better than that of Burke himself, commenting, 'The strange means by which the wretch made his money are scarce more disgusting than the eager curiosity with which the public have licked up all the carrion details of this business.'

Robert Louis Stevenson (1850–94) wrote a short story called 'The Body Snatcher' in 1884, which is based on the Burke and Hare story and features characters from Dr Knox's practice, with a suitably macabre ending in which two of Knox's pupils steal a body from a graveyard: 'As two vultures may swoop down upon a dying lamb, Fettes and MacFarlane were let loose upon a grave in that green and quiet resting-place. The wife of a farmer was to be rooted from her grave at midnight and carried, dead and naked, to be exposed to that last curiosity of the anatomist'. Having removed the body from the grave, Fettes and MacFarlane discover, to their horror, that it is in fact the body of a man called Gray which they had previously dissected.

THE ITALIAN BOY

A particularly scandalous instance of bodysnatching occurred in November 1831, in a case which became known as 'The Italian Boy'. Two resurrection men called John Bishop and Thomas Williams lured the child, wrongly identified as Carlo Ferrari from Piedmont, to a house they were renting in Nova Scotia Gardens, Bethnal Green. The area has since been redeveloped and lies to the north-east of St Leonard's church, Shoreditch, in an area which in 1831 was noted for its criminality and was later occupied by Columbia Market. In fact, the boy was not Italian. He was a young cattle drover on his way from Lincoln to or from Smithfield market and was looking for a night's lodgings. He had been picked up by Bishop and Williams from a Smithfield pub, The Bell. When he reached Nova Scotia Gardens the boy was drugged with rum and laudanum, a form of opium then available across the counter from any chemist. Leaving the drugs to take effect, Bishop and Williams then went for a drink to a nearby pub, The Feathers, and returned to find the boy in a coma. They lowered him into a well by a rope attached to his feet and waited while his small body contorted in its vain struggle for life. Finally the boy died.

The body of a previously healthy child was exceptionally valuable to a teaching hospital, but when Bishop and Williams took the body to Guy's Hospital they were turned away. They then approached King's College School of Anatomy in the Strand, demanding 12 guineas. They accepted 9 but Dr Richard Partridge, Professor of Anatomy, was suspicious and called the police. Bishop and Williams were arrested and charged with wilful murder, and a search of their premises at Nova Scotia Gardens produced evidence of other murders. Bishop and Williams eventually confessed to three similar offences, all against rough sleepers and one of them involving a very small child.

The two men were hanged at Newgate on 5 December 1831 before a rejoicing crowd estimated at 30,000. Appropriately, their bodies were sent for dissection: Bishop's to King's College and Williams's to the theatre of anatomy off the Haymarket where, over the next two days, their corpses were viewed by large crowds of sightseers.

15

REPLACING PROPER CHARLEYS WITH OLD BILL

MAGISTRATES: 'LOW, NEEDY AND MERCENARY FOOLS'

In 1740, Thomas de Veil established an office on Bow Street, Covent Garden, on what was to become the site of the world's most famous magistrates' court, which continued to administer justice until it was finally closed in July 2006. Its final case concerned a vagrant, as had many of its cases from de Veil's time. De Veil was a Justice of the Peace, whose origins were lost in the mists of medieval history, but unlike his predecessors he received a salary (from the secret service fund) which made him the first stipendiary professional magistrate or, as they are now called, district judges (Magistrates' Courts).

He had been appointed to the post by the Lord Chancellor with instructions to end the corruption which had infected the magistracy, particularly in the Covent Garden area, the centre of London's criminal underworld. 'Basket justices' openly paraded their willingness to accept gifts (bribes) in baskets that they carried in return for turning a blind eye to the prostitution and protection rackets that plagued that benighted corner of London. De Veil described such magistrates as:

Low, needy and mercenary fools who subsist on their commissions. They are hated and dreaded by the common people who fancy they have greater powers than they really have ... they are as much afraid of being carried before his worship as the people of Paris fear the Bastille or the inhabitants of Lisbon the Inquisition.

De Veil was a soldier of fortune of French ancestry who had fought in the Duke of Marlborough's armies in the early years of the century. His career as magistrate made a promising start when he was stabbed by a fellow magistrate called Webster, whom de Veil had reported to the Lord Chancellor for corruption. For this injury he received compensation and the following year further indications of his success followed when he was attacked by a gang of robbers whom he was bringing to justice, one of them being a solicitor.

De Veil was knighted for his services in 1744 and when he died in 1747, his body was removed from his Bow Street home early in the morning to escape the attention of the many enemies he had made amongst the criminal classes.

TOM JONES IN BOW STREET

De Veil's successor was Henry Fielding (1707–54) who had already enjoyed a controversial career as a playwright and satirist. He had so offended Prime Minister Robert Walpole with his biting theatrical satires on the venality and corruption of the government that in 1737 the prime minister had passed the Theatrical Licensing Act, which made the Lord Chamberlain responsible for authorising all stage productions. This Act drove Fielding into novel writing which, being a new form of literature, escaped the Lord Chamberlain's censure. The result was the first major English novel, *Tom Jones*.

Fielding owed his appointment to the post of Chief Metropolitan Magistrate to William Pitt the Elder, an old school friend who was largely responsible for the fall of Walpole and his replacement. This act of nepotism was to prove decisive in the development of an effective and honest judicial system.

Fielding continued for a while to make use of the services of thief-takers who were, in effect, the heirs of Jonathan Wild, but he concentrated on the development of a corps of trustworthy constables, eight of whom he inherited from de Veil. In addition there were the Charleys, who originated in the reign of Charles II (hence the name) and consisted mainly of elderly ex-soldiers. Described by Fielding as 'Poor, old decrepit people' they have given us the expression 'Proper Charleys' to signify someone who is of little use. Fielding appointed as his chief constable a man called

Blind John Fielding: scourge of criminals.

Saunders Welch, a product of the Aylesbury workhouse who had become a prosperous grocer and shared Fielding's views on how to rid Covent Garden of criminals. Welch and his band of constable were the forerunners of the Bow Street Runners and hence precursors of the Metropolitan Police. They were paid from reward money gained by recovering stolen property.

Fielding placed advertisements in newspapers, which asked citizens who were the victims of crimes to approach him with details of their losses and invited these victims to view people who had been arrested by the constables to identify possible culprits. In 1753 Fielding was approached by the Duke of Newcastle, soon to be prime minister, who asked him to deal with the gangs who were terrorising the Covent Garden area. Fielding recruited a special force of constables who captured seven of the principal culprits after a ferocious battle so that, in Fielding's words, 'this hellish society were almost utterly extirpated'. Shortly after this triumph Fielding, a victim of dropsy, gout and exhaustion, retired and set off for Lisbon, whose climate he hoped would restore him to health. He died there in October 1754 and is buried in that city.

'A SET OF BRAVE FELLOWS'

Henry Fielding's successor was his brother John Fielding, who had been blind since 1740 as a result of an accident sustained while serving in the Royal Navy. John's zeal, if anything, exceeded Henry's. In *The Public Advertiser* he placed an advertisement inviting victims of crime to contact him, upon which he would 'immediately despatch a set of brave fellows in pursuit who have long been engaged for such purposes, on a quarter of an hour's notice'. He also instituted both foot patrols and patrols mounted on horseback, the latter being equipped with firearms to deal with highwaymen. The Bow Street Runners' most notable achievement, in 1820, was the apprehension of the Cato Street Conspirators, a bunch of foolish desperadoes who planned to murder the cabinet and take over the government. One Runner was killed and the conspirators were the last to be sentenced to be hung, drawn and quartered for treason, though a merciful executioner made sure they were dead before he decapitated them.

Exection of the Cato Street conspirators outside Newgate: coffins at the ready.

The work of the Fieldings was so successful that in 1785 the government introduced a Bill to create a system of paid commissioners to supervise crime prevention and detection throughout the capital. It failed only because the Lord Mayor feared that it would interfere with the exclusive jurisdiction which the City exercised within the Square Mile, but it was the precursor of the work of Sir Robert Peel who, as Home Secretary, created the Metropolitan Police. 'The Met'

Cato Street conspirators interrupted by Bow Street Runners.

are not, however, the world's oldest police force. That honour goes to the Thames River Police, a private force set up by dockland merchants to protect their ships and cargoes from thieves and now, of course, absorbed into the Metropolitan Police.

In 1829, Sir Robert Peel persuaded Parliament to pass the Act that set up the Metropolitan Police. In his former capacity as Chief Secretary for Ireland, Peel had set up the Royal Irish Constabulary to prevent civil disorder and the Lord Mayor was appeased by allowing the City to have its own police force, which it created in 1839 and which remains independent of the Metropolitan Police. The Bow Street Runners maintained their independence for ten years and were then themselves absorbed into the Metropolitan force, as was the Thames River service. In 1836 the Bow Street horse patrols became the mounted division of the Metropolitan Police, forfeiting their firearms in the process.

FOURTEEN-HOUR DAYS
FOR A GUINEA A WEEK

On Saturday, 26 September 1829, the 3,000 new recruits assembled in the grounds of the Foundling Hospital, Holborn, where they received their uniform of dark blue coats, trousers and top hats.

The following Tuesday they set out on their new beats, replacing the Charleys, though a few of these survived into the 1870s. The new force was supervised in its early days by two commissioners, one an ex-soldier and one a barrister. There was a strong desire to emphasise that the new force was not the military under another name, so the uniform was deliberately unmilitary in style and the constables were equipped with truncheons rather than firearms, though inspectors in the early days were allowed to carry small pistols in their pockets. The work was arduous, with 14-hour days, and the pay modest at a guinea (£1.05) a week, which may account for the fact that, of the 3,000 recruits who set out in September 1829, three quarters had left or been dismissed within four years.

COPPERS, BOBBIES AND THE OLD BILL

The truncheons were soon encircled with a band of copper on which was engraved W IV R to represent William IV, who became king in 1830. The truncheon was thus a symbol of the authority which resided ultimately in the monarch and accounted for two expressions which have passed down to the present day. William IV was referred to in the press as 'Silly Billy' or 'Old Bill' and the name 'Bill' came to be attached to the new force as did the word 'copper' in reference to the copper ring. The names 'Bobby' or, in Ireland, 'Peelers', derived from the Home Secretary who created the force.

Further Acts of Parliament authorised boroughs to establish their own police forces on the Metropolitan model, some of them very small. Southwold in Suffolk, for example, had one constable. Detectives appeared in the 1840s and in 1861 the blue lamp first appeared outside police stations, an exception being made for the station in Bow Street, Covent Garden. This had a white lamp to spare the sensibilities of Queen Victoria who, on her frequent visits to the opera house, did not wish to be reminded of the Blue Room at Windsor in which Prince Albert had died in 1861. The police station closed in 2002, four years before the adjacent magistrates' court.

The new force was to act as a model for other police forces throughout the world with one major exception; foreign forces were routinely provided with firearms from their early days. During the Second World War, police guarding the royal family and Downing Street were issued with firearms, but the introduction of firearms to other officers had to wait until the 1960s, following the murder of three police officers in 1966 by Harry Roberts. Each police service now has a firearms unit containing officers specially trained in their use. Fewer than one in five officers are authorised to use firearms and, except in an emergency, the use of firearms has to be authorised in advance by an officer of the rank of inspector or above.

PRESTON NORTH END *vs.* QPR

Patterns of crime changed as the new police forces became established in the nineteenth century. Burglary and murder peaked in the 1860s, while major financial frauds increased

in number as commercial activities offered greater rewards to fraudsters like George Hudson (1800–71), the 'Railway King', who defrauded investors in his highly speculative ventures. In 1886 the Metropolitan Police had to deal with its first case of football hooliganism involving a fierce confrontation between supporters of Preston North End and Queen's Park Rangers, shortly after the foundation of QPR. In 1898 they were called to a violent brawl in the Old Kent road on the August bank holiday, the participants fuelled by drink. Thus were patterns set for the centuries which followed!

16

PANOPTICONS AND MISGUIDED REFORMS

LOCK 'EM UP

As the Bloody Code was dismantled in the early part of the nineteenth century, alternative methods of punishment were required. The pillory was last used in 1837 and transportation to the American colonies ceased after the War of Independence, though convicts continued to be sent to Australia until the 1860s. It is thus no coincidence that so many of our prisons date from Victorian times, since it was from the 1830s that prison came to be viewed not only as a means of detaining prisoners prior to trial and execution but as a punishment in its own right. The construction of the Victorian prisons (many of them built by John Nash, the later designer of Regent's Park and Regent Street) also coincided with the development of a philosophy of imprisonment whose aim was to reform offenders rather than merely detain them.

'DISORDERLY POOR' AND ORPHANS

There were exceptions. Bridewell Prison in the City of London was established in 1553 in a former royal palace between Fleet Street and the Thames in what is now Bridewell Place, the site now occupied by a Crowne Plaza Hotel. It gave its name to other similar establishments in towns and cities throughout England, and in London it served two purposes: the detention of the 'disorderly poor' (a kind of Tudor workhouse or house of correction), and a more charitable purpose of housing and training homeless and orphaned children. It was governed jointly with Bethlem Hospital (known as Bedlam) which cared for the insane and was then located in Bishopsgate on the present site of Liverpool Street station.

Visitors were allowed and medical care was available. Prison reformer John Howard praised its regime when he visited it in 1789, though from the 1770s prison reformers argued that mixing children with the disorderly poor corrupted the children. When the Gordon Rioters set fire to Newgate in 1780 they left the bridewell buildings intact. It was closed in 1855 but its educational facilities moved to King Edward's School, Witley, in Surrey.

TOLBOOTHS

In Scotland, the function of bridewells was performed by tolbooths, which were the principal building of a town or city. They housed the town council and its records, as well as serving as a courthouse and prison. Scotland's most famous tolbooth was that of Edinburgh. It was known as The Heart of Midlothian and features prominently in Sir Walter Scott's novel of that name. It was also used as a place of execution until its demolition in 1817, when Scott purchased its main entrance to incorporate into his neo-Gothic home at Abbotsford, near Melrose. The original site of the tolbooth is marked by a brass plate set into granite stones in Edinburgh's Parliament Square, close to the cathedral of St Giles, and its former unofficial title survives in the name of one of Scotland's leading football clubs, Heart of Midlothian FC.

THE PANOPTICON EXPERIMENT

One of the advocates of using prisons to reform rather than detain was the utilitarian philosopher Jeremy Bentham (1748–1832), who applied to every government act the principle of utility: would it bring more pleasure than pain or, in plainer terms, would it do more good than harm. He argued that 'punishment is mischief: all punishment is itself evil ... it ought only to be admitted in as far as it promises to exclude some greater evil'. He divided prisons into three categories:

The House of Safe Custody was to hold debtors and those awaiting trial (the latter would now be held in a remand prison).

The second was a penitentiary, which would accommodate those serving short sentences for relatively minor offences.

The third was the Black House, for those serving longer sentences.

Jeremy Bentham advocated the construction of panopticon (literally 'all-seeing') prisons for the last two categories.

PANOPTICON PRISONS

These prisons were designed with a central, circular tower from which the wings radiated, each wing containing a number of cells. Prisoners would be isolated in their cells while visible to prison warders via a system of mirrors from the central tower. The cells would be lit by daylight, but the central tower would have no external windows, which would make it relatively dark so the warders could see into the cells but not vice versa. Consequently no prisoner would know whether he was being observed ('each person should actually be in that predicament during every instant of time'), thus engendering a feeling of insecurity amongst the inmates which, it was thought, would do them good. Moreover, magistrates and other prison inspectors could 'quickly inspect large numbers of prisoners without having to come near to such disgusting and repugnant objects as the prisoners themselves'.

Under this system, no communication was permitted between prisoners in the hope that solitude would encourage them to reflect upon their past errors and mend their ways. At this time, the 'miasmatic' theory of disease transmission was prevalent and held that all disease was transmitted through foul air, and Bentham and others extended this belief to bad behaviour, believing that criminal habits could be passed from one convict to another through the air. There is some truth in the idea that prisons act as 'universities of crime', but air is no longer held to blame.

In its extreme form, prisoners, besides not being allowed to converse, were not even allowed to see one another. This was known as the 'separate' system under which, during exercise periods or even in chapel, prisoners would wear masks which gave a very narrow field of vision and prevented them from seeing each other. Contact with prison staff was conducted via conversation tubes. In the old prison at Lincoln, partitions were placed between each seat in the chapel which prevented prisoners from seeing one another.

Bentham described these processes as 'a new mode of obtaining power of mind over mind', which would thereby influence criminals for the better. The words 'Big Brother', however, also come to mind.

RULES OF SEVERITY AND ECONOMY

Bentham argued that imprisonment should 'not be accompanied by bodily suffering', which ruled out the former practices of

The treadwheel in use.

starvation and putting prisoners in irons. On the other hand, the Rule of Severity prescribed that prison conditions should be no better than those endured by innocent but poor citizens who had their freedom. This in turn led to the Rule of Economy, which meant that as a further measure, prisoners were expected to work for their keep if they wanted a diet other than stale bread and water, which was barely enough to keep them alive. This might mean unravelling tarred ropes (a penalty undergone by Oscar Wilde), operating a treadmill or raising a weight by winding a crank handle as many as 10,000 times, which could be made tougher by tightening the screws that governed the effort required to turn the handle. It is from this process that the word 'screw' came to be applied to prison officers.

'MAKE THE BRAWNY NAVVY CRY LIKE A CHILD'

One of the prisons in which the silent and separate systems were tested to destruction was Pentonville, which opened in 1842 and was designed on panopticon principles. A Trappist monastery would have been riotous in comparison with the Pentonville regime which was embraced enthusiastically by its first governor, Sir Joshua Jebb (1793–1863). Prison officers wore padded shoes and when prisoners left their cells they wore hoods. Work involved hard labour such as breaking stones for road making, and the chaplain of Preston Prison reported enthusiastically that a few months under this regime would 'render a prisoner strangely impressible. The chaplain can then make the brawny navvy cry like a child; he can work his feelings in any way he pleases'. Several cases of insanity resulted from these regimes, which was presumably not the outcome intended.

MILLBANK PRISON

The first prison to be built by the Home Office was at Millbank. It was designed on panopticon principles and opened in 1821 with a capacity of over 1,000 prisoners. Upon arrival prisoners were bathed, had their hair cut, or shaved if sentenced to penal

Millbank Prison: now the site of Tate Britain.

servitude (hard labour), and issued with the uniform decorated with arrows familiar from films and comics. Prisoners spent the first six months in the separate system, having no contact at all with other prisoners and exercising for 1 hour each day. After that they moved to the silent system, so they saw other prisoners but weren't allowed to talk to them. Men and women were separated and the inmates were taught tailoring and shoemaking, making uniforms and boots for the military. The diet was good, with a plentiful supply of meat, vegetables, milk, bread and potatoes. This was better than many poor people could afford outside the prison, so a press campaign against the 'fattening house', as the prison became known, led to a reduction in the diet.

Unfortunately the site of the prison was a former marsh and many prisoners became ill, with several dying. In the 1850s, despite the diet, each prisoner at Millbank was ill on average four times a year, whereas at Brixton it was one quarter of prisoners each year. Because of its poor health record, Millbank became an assembly point where convicts were briefly held before transportation or dispersal to other prisons. The prison closed in 1890 and the site, once properly drained, became the site of Tate Britain which incorporates many of Millbank's materials in its own structure.

THE HULKS

In 1776, old warships were moored in the Thames and the Medway to hold prisoners awaiting transportation to America during the War of Independence. Their use continued until the 1850s for those awaiting transportation to Australia, many of Nelson's battle fleet ending their days in this ignominious manner. Convicts would be taken to them from Newgate in carts, where onlookers would gather to shout and jeer at the chained prisoners as they took their first steps to a new life.

Magwitch in Charles Dickens's *Great Expectations* suffered this fate but returned to meet his end. In *David Copperfield*, Dickens sent Uriah Heap to Australia for his crimes, though in the same book Wilkins Micawber is allowed to emigrate to the colony of his own free will hoping, as ever, that 'Something will turn up'. Later in the century, these and other ships were used to hold people suffering from smallpox in quarantine to prevent the disease from spreading to those of the population who had declined vaccination.

A hulk awaits its inmates.

There are at present 139 prisons in the United Kingdom, including seven private prisons run by companies like G4S. They hold over 80,000 prisoners, the prison population peaking in December 2011 at just over 88,000. The prisons briefly described below are amongst the better known.

DARTMOOR PRISON

Dartmoor Prison opened in 1809 to accommodate prisoners from the Napoleonic Wars, to whom were later added American prisoners taken in the war of 1812. It is built on land owned by the Duchy of Cornwall and as such provides some of the income for the duke, better known as the Prince of Wales. At one time it held 6,500 American sailors who, following the end of the war, grew impatient at delays in sending them home and rioted, resulting in 271 deaths.

Dartmoor Prison, Princetown. (Courtesy of Matilda Richards)

It reopened in 1851 as a civilian prison but, in 1917, it was used as a holding centre for conscientious objectors who refused to serve in the First World War. It operated, effectively, as an open prison in which inmates wore their own clothing and could visit the nearby village. In 1920 it became a prison for serious offenders.

It is now used as a Category C prison for non-violent offenders, many guilty of white-collar crime such as fraud. It entered the headlines in December 1966 when the notorious Kray twins arranged the escape of a prisoner with a history of violence called Frank Mitchell, known as 'The Mad Axeman' because of one of his earlier exploits. The Krays appear to have done this to show that they were above the law and to orchestrate a campaign for Mitchell's release. When Mitchell started to make demands on the Krays and refused to co-operate with their plans, they had him shot.

DURHAM PRISON

Construction of the present Durham Prison began in 1809 and it was long used as a Category A prison to house the most dangerous prisoners of both sexes. It has had a substantial number of notorious criminals (including Rose West and Myra Hindley) in its female wings; and in its male wings it has accommodated Ronald Kray and his associate 'Mad' Frankie Fraser, as well as Charlie and Eddie Richardson from the South London Richardson gang, the rivals of the Krays in the 1960s. Ian Brady was also an inmate before being transferred to Ashworth psychiatric hospital in Maghull, Merseyside.

STRANGEWAYS PRISON

Strangeways in Manchester was completed in 1869 to a design of the celebrated Victorian architect Alfred Waterhouse, who also designed the Natural History Museum in London. It was based on a panopticon design with some variations and was one of the few prisons to have a permanent gallows, where 100 executions took place before hanging was abolished. At Strangeways, Albert

Pierrepoint carried out the quickest hanging ever recorded when, in May 1951, he hanged the murderer James Inglis within 7 seconds of his leaving the cell.

In April 1990, the prison was the scene of a riot which lasted for twenty-five days and resulted in injuries to 147 prison staff and 47 prisoners. Lurid accounts given by prisoners and eagerly repeated by the media about the execution of inmates by other prisoners were widely reported but turned out to be fanciful; one prisoner and one prison officer died, the latter from heart failure. The prison was extensively rebuilt after the riots and is now a high-security Category A prison. Its residents have included the footballer Joey Barton; the Moors murderer Ian Brady; Dale Cregan, the murderer of two policewomen; Mark Bridger who murdered April Jones; Dr Harold Shipman and the suffragette Christabel Pankhurst.

OPEN PRISONS

Open prisons are normally used for prisoners who present a low risk of attempting to escape or of becoming violent. Some of these people are white-collar criminals convicted of offences like fraud, and others are prisoners who are coming to the end of long sentences for whom an open prison is seen as a halfway house leading to their release. Two of the better-known open prisons are Ford in Sussex, and North Sea Camp in Lincolnshire, which was home to Jeffrey Archer while he was serving a sentence for perjury.

In 2006 it was revealed that seventy inmates, including three murderers serving the last three years of their sentences, had absconded from Ford open prison in twelve months. In 2009, it was reported that the prison was open in the wrong direction: poor security systems made it possible for burglars to break into the prison to steal equipment from workshops. It was also revealed that inmates were leaving the prison at night to purchase alcohol. Two years later a journalist broke into the prison and published details of its lax security. Its former inmates have included the footballer George Best; the insurance fraudster

Lord Brocket; and Ernest Saunders, convicted in connection with the Guinness takeover of the Distillers company. Saunders was released early on the grounds that he was suffering from Alzheimer's disease, a condition from which, most unusually, he made a good recovery.

WORMWOOD SCRUBS

Wormwood Scrubs Prison is built on the largest open space in the London borough of Hammersmith in West London. Construction began in 1874 and much of the prison was built by prisoners from other gaols who were approaching their release date. During the Second World War the prisoners were removed and the building was occupied by the security services, MI5 and MI6. Former inmates have included the spy George Blake (who escaped, see page 107); the fraudster Horatio Bottomley; popular musicians Pete Doherty and Keith Richards; and Oscar Wilde's paramour and nemesis Lord Alfred Douglas. It is a Grade II listed building on account of its distinctive gatehouse which, for that reason, is frequently used in films and TV programmes when someone is being released from prison. These have included *Billy Liar*, *The Sweeney*, *Minder*, *Steptoe and Son* (whose premises were nearby) and, of course, *Porridge*.

SLADE PRISON

The most famous prison is undoubtedly *Porridge*'s Slade Prison, the unwilling residents of which include Norman Stanley Fletcher and his friends Lenny Godber, Bunny Warren, 'Horrible' Ives, Black Jock and genial Harry Grout, the prison godfather on whose behalf the governor runs the prison with the assistance of naive Mr Barrowclough and tough Mr Mackay. The comedy series, written by Dick Clement and Ian La Frenais, succeeds in imparting humour and congeniality to the characters one would normally shun. Those familiar with prison life have informed the author (who served for sixteen years as a magistrate) that the relationship between Mr Mackay and the inmates is very close to the truth. The viewer was encouraged to believe that Slade Prison was somewhere in the north, perhaps near Carlisle. The refusal of the Home Office to allow any filming of real prisons obliged the producers to use the frontage of the former St Albans Prison as the entrance to Slade, though later in the series the exterior of Maidstone Prison was used. The series was filmed between 1974 and 1977, made the reputations of many of the actors involved (David Jason had a brief run in the series) and is still regularly shown as repeats.

17

'ON GOING TO SEE A MAN HANGED'

'NOTHING BUT RIBALDRY, LEVITY, DRUNKENNESS AND FLAUNTING VICE'

On 6 July 1840, two young writers attended the execution of a young valet called Francois Courvoisier outside the gate of Newgate Prison. Courvoisier had killed his master, Lord William Russell. Charles Dickens, who had a balcony seat, was there as a journalist and the other writer, whom Dickens observed in the throng numbering tens of thousands, was William Thackeray, who had been invited to attend by his friend Richard Monkton Milnes in the hope that the writer would join Milnes in campaigning for the abolition of the death penalty. Thackeray left an account of the event in his essay 'On Going to see a man hanged', a powerful argument against public hanging, even though there was no doubt of Courvoisier's guilt. He concluded, 'I have been abetting an act of frightful wickedness and violence ... I pray that it may soon be out of the power of any man in England to witness such a hideous and degrading sight'. Dickens, in his article for the *Daily News* wrote, 'I did not see one token in all the immense crowd of any one emotion suitable to the occasion; nothing but ribaldry, levity, drunkenness and flaunting vice in fifty other shapes'. Dickens added that the only evidence of decorum in the entire process was the cry of 'Hats off!' as the executioner took the lever which opened the trap door and ended a life.

Both men thereafter campaigned against public executions and twenty-eight years later, after much ink had been consumed, executions were moved inside Newgate in 1868. Two weeks after the event Thackeray, still distressed by the memory, wrote:

> I have the man's face continually before my eyes; I can see Mr Ketch at this moment, with an easy air, taking his rope from his pocket; I feel myself shamed and degraded at the brutal curiosity that took me to that brutal sight; and I pray to God Almighty to cause this disgraceful sin to pass from among us, and to cleanse our land of blood.

It is perhaps no coincidence that the ending of public executions was accompanied by the development of a new genre of literature which concentrated on sensational, preferably bloody, crimes. The *Illustrated Police News* began publication in the 1860s and continued until 1938, taking advantage of improvements in printing techniques with illustrations of crimes, criminals and crime scenes. Local newspapers quickly realised that they gained readers (and advertising) by featuring sensational local crimes. Later in the century, more sophisticated stories of crime emerged for a more discerning and literate public, the most famous being Arthur Conan Doyle's tales of Sherlock Holmes, who made his first appearance in *A Study in Scarlet* in 1887, the *Illustrated Police News* itself being mentioned in some of the stories. Holmes survived the attempt by his author to drown him in 1893 in a struggle to the death with his arch-enemy Professor Moriarty at the Reichenbach Falls. By popular demand, Conan Doyle rescued him and Holmes continued to solve crimes until 1927. Now the Reichenbach Falls, near Meiringen in Switzerland, boasts a Sherlock Holmes museum.

THE NEWGATE CALENDAR

Before the arrival of the *Illustrated Police News*, Newgate had generated its own cruder accounts of criminals and went on to spawn more prison literature than any other prison in the world. This was partly due to its antiquity, stretching from the twelfth century to the dawn of the twentieth century, but it is also due to the existence of the *Newgate Calendar*. This was originally a record kept by the Keeper of Newgate of the names of those entering the prison: a prison register. However it soon came to encompass a wide variety of publications, which included accounts (often fanciful) of the trials and misdeeds of Newgate's inmates, with separate volumes on highwaymen, pirates and final speeches from the scaffold. In the 1820s, two lawyers called Andrew Knapp and William Baldwin published a selection of these works in four volumes entitled *The Newgate Calendar Comprising Interesting Memoirs of the Most Notorious Characters*. They sold well to a reading public hungry for sensational material of this kind, and provided the raw material for the accounts of other minor authors as well as inspiring authors like John Gay, William Thackeray and Charles Dickens.

THE BEGGAR'S OPERA

The first major literary work based upon Newgate was *The Beggar's Opera*, first produced in 1728. The author, John Gay (1685–1732) was born in Barnstaple, Devon, but was drawn to London where his facility with words earned him the friendship of Jonathan Swift, Alexander Pope and Richard Steele, the editor of *The Spectator*. The principal character of *The Beggar's Opera* is Peachum, a receiver of stolen goods and informant, clearly based upon Jonathan Wild who had been hanged three years earlier. Other characters include the gallant highwayman Macheath, Lucy Lockit, the Newgate gaoler's daughter, and Polly Peachum, Lucy's rival in love for Macheath. The sympathetic portrayal of a criminal like Macheath was popular with the crowds who attended the performances but offended the authorities, as did Gay's critical portrayal of Walpole's government. Walpole, in retaliation, deprived Gay of his comfortable and profitable sinecure as commissioner of lotteries, but the opera made Gay a rich man. In 1928, 200 years after Gay's work was first produced, Bertold Brecht produced his own work based upon it featuring the character of 'Mack the Knife', the ruthless but attractive and successful robber.

THE NEWGATE NOVEL

Following the creation of the office of Lord Chamberlain in 1737 to censor stage productions, future fictional accounts of life in Newgate would take the form of the novel. Daniel Defoe (1660–1731) had been briefly gaoled in Newgate for his pamphlet 'The Shortest Way with Dissenters' and drew on the experience for his novel *Moll Flanders*, the eponymous heroine being born in Newgate and spending much of the novel in and out of the gaol. Defoe also produced his own account of *The Life and Actions of the late Jonathan Wild* within three years of Wild's death. Henry Fielding drew on his experiences of Newgate and the justice system in his novel *Amelia*, the character of Amelia herself being based upon Fielding's much-loved wife Charlotte. Amelia's husband is imprisoned in Newgate on a false charge but learns, while there, that Amelia has been shorn of her inheritance by a dishonest lawyer who is duly executed.

William Godwin (1756–1836) is usually remembered as the husband of Mary Wollstonecraft, author of the *A Vindication of the Rights of Woman* and father of Mary Shelley, but he also wrote a novel called *Caleb Williams: or Things As They Are*, a crime novel which makes many references to the state of the prison system. Harrison Ainsworth (1805–82) was one of the most popular writers of his age and based novels on Jack Sheppard, Jonathan Wild, the Witches of Pendle and Dick Turpin, whose entirely fictional ride to York (where Turpin was in fact hanged) was invented by the writer. Ainsworth's better-known contemporary was Edward Bulwer-Lytton (1803–73) who is best known for *The Last Days of Pompeii*. In his lifetime he made his fortune from Newgate novels, including *Paul Clifford*, which opens with one of the best-known and later hackneyed sentences in English literature: 'It was a dark and stormy night'.

William Makepeace Thackeray (1811–63) had reservations about the depiction of criminals by Ainsworth and Bulwer-Lytton and wrote the novel *Catherine*, based upon a woman who had been burned at the stake in 1726 for the murder of her husband, intending it as a corrective. It appeared in serial form in *Fraser's Magazine* in 1839–40 and proved very popular, though not in the way Thackeray intended, since most readers were drawn to the strong and ill-served character of Catherine. The year that *Catherine* finished publication, 1840, was also the year that Thackeray saw Courvoisier hanged, an execution which was the more controversial because it was argued in the trial that Courvoisier had read Ainsworth's *Jack Sheppard* and been moved to commit his crime by the events described in the novel.

CHARLES DICKENS

Charles Dickens named his eldest son, Edward Bulwer Lytton Dickens, after his friend and fellow novelist and drew on his own experiences of the legal system in many of his novels. After his spell in the blacking factory and the release of his hapless father from the Marshalsea (having paid his debt from a legacy left to him by

Charles Dickens late in life.

his mother), Charles was articled to a solicitor and learned shorthand, becoming first a parliamentary and legal reporter and later a journalist with the *Morning Chronicle*. In *Sketches by Boz*, he wrote an account of a visit to Newgate and visited the chapel where he wrote of:

> The condemned pew; a huge black pen in which the wretched people who are singled out for death are placed on the Sunday preceding their execution, to hear prayers for their own souls, to join in the responses of their own burial service and to listen to an address urging themselves, while there is yet time, to 'turn and flee from the wrath to come'.

He saw almost thirty awaiting execution, including an elderly man and a boy under 14 (though it was normal by this time for young criminals to have their sentences commuted) and fourteen child pickpockets 'drawn up in a line for our inspection, not one redeeming feature among them, not a glance of honesty not a wink or anything expressive of anything but the gallows or the hulks'. He also witnessed the solitary system in use in Philadelphia during one of his visits to the USA, and saw the prisoners wearing black hoods to prevent any contact with others: 'he never looks upon a human countenance or hears a human voice. He is a man buried alive to be dug out in the slow round of years and in the meantime dead to torturing anxieties and horrible despair'. One prisoner, after eleven years of this solitary treatment, would say nothing but would only 'stare at his hands and pick the flesh upon his fingers'. Some prisoners, upon release, could not hold the pen steadily to sign the discharge book and could only lean upon the prison wall and some had become deaf. Dickens drew upon these observations to describe Old Dorrit's inability to cope with life outside the Marshalsea when he was discharged.

'THE CURSE OF ALL ITS VICTIMS PAST, AND PRESENT AND TO COME'

References to the legal and prison system abound in his work. In *David Copperfield*, David is articled to the firm of Spenlow & Jorkins in Doctors Commons, a College of Law (in effect an Inn of Court) described as 'a cosy, dosy, old fashioned, time forgotten sleepy headed little family party'. Doctors Commons, which had once numbered Sir Thomas More amongst its members, was by Dickens's time on its last legs. It closed in 1865 and its former premises are marked by a plaque in Queen Victoria Street. Spenlow tells David that the best kind of legal business is:

> A good case of a disputed will where there was a neat little estate of thirty or forty thousand pounds was perhaps the best of all. In such a case, he said, not only were there very pretty pickings in the way of arguments at every stage of the proceedings ... but, the costs being pretty sure to come out of the proceeds of the estate at last, both sides went at it in a lively and spirited manner, and expense was no consideration.

Dickens also sends David Copperfield to investigate the separate system in a prison, which leads David to comment on the prison diet:

> I wondered whether it occurred to anybody that there was a striking contrast between these plentiful repasts of choice quality and the dinners, not to say of paupers but of soldiers, sailors, labourers, the great bulk of the honest working community, of whom not one in five hundred ever dined half so well.

Dickens's cynical view of the legal system found its most strident expression in *Bleak House*, where the legal obfuscations of the case of Jarndyce *v.* Jarndyce eventually consume the entire value of the estate, much of the action taking place in the offices of the sinister lawyer Tulkinghorn in Lincoln's Inn and the Court of Chancery.

However Dickens's most vivid use of his knowledge of the legal system are to be found in *Oliver Twist*, especially in the scene where Oliver visits his exploiter Fagin in Newgate. As Fagin hears the sentence of death pronounced for his crimes at the Old Bailey, he hears 'a peal of joy from the populace outside, greeting the news that he would die on Monday'. Oliver visits Fagin in the condemned cell and sees his face 'retaining no human expression but rage and terror', with no sign of remorse. As he leaves the prison, Oliver sees that 'everything told of life and animation but one dark cluster of objects in the centre of all – the black stage, the cross beam, the rope and all the hideous apparatus of death'.

Other prisoners attract Dickens's sympathy. In *The Old Curiosity Shop*, the errand boy Kit Nubbles is framed by the evil dwarf Quilp and sent to prison, but Dickens assures the reader that Kit is lodged 'apart from the masses of prisoners because he was not supposed to be utterly depraved and irreclaimable'.

In *Great Expectations* Dickens returns to the Old Bailey, in the form of Pip, to witness Magwitch in the dock hearing the death sentence pronounced upon him for returning from transportation for life. Pip holds Magwitch's hand as, 'Penned in the dock, as I stood outside it at the corner with his hand in mine, were the two-and-thirty men and women: some defiant, some stricken with terror, some sobbing and weeping, some covering their faces, some staring gloomily about. There had been shrieks from among the women convicts but they had been stilled and a hush had succeeded.' Magwitch, who is mortally ill, tells the judge, 'My lord I have received my sentence of death from the Almighty but I bow to yours'.

Barnaby Rudge: a Tale of the Riots of Eighty revolves around the Gordon Riots and, in particular, the attack upon Newgate Prison and the Old Bailey. The simpleton Barnaby Rudge is inveigled into taking part in the riots, sent to Newgate, released by the mob and, having been recaptured and returned to Newgate, is redeemed at the eleventh hour. Barnaby is the subject of one of Hablot Knight Browne's most famous illustrations of Dickens, fettered and puzzled in the dark condemned cell. Hugh the ostler is not so fortunate. Like his mother, a gypsy, Hugh is hanged outside Newgate but is defiant and as he approaches the scaffold he cries, 'Upon these human shambles I, who never raised a hand in prayer till now, call down the wrath of God! On that black tree, of which I am the ripened fruit, I do invoke the curse of all its victims past, and present and to come.'

In the twentieth century, these earlier authors have been joined by the late John Mortimer's creation, the barrister Horace Rumpole of *Rumpole of the Bailey*, with his only moderately successful practice.

Rumpole is a source of endless disappointment to his critical wife, 'She who must be obeyed'. In earlier centuries she would no doubt have been subjected to a spell on the ducking stool as an inveterate scold. Rumpole, with his garrulous tendency to endlessly quote Shakespeare in Pomeroy's wine bar (better known as El Vino's) would, the present author suspects, have emptied many a saloon bar.

18

THINGS CAN
ONLY GET
BETTER

THE STATE OF THE PRISONS

As Jeremy Bentham and those who shared his views were reforming the design of prisons, others, including Elizabeth Fry (1780–1845) were attempting to make the prisons more humane. Her appearance on the £5 note in 2002 was in recognition of her critical role in this process, but she was not the first to turn her thoughts to reform of the system. Pride of place in that respect must go to John Howard (1726–1790).

Howard was born in London to a prosperous family and brought up in Cardington, Bedfordshire, after his mother died when he was 5 years old. At the age of 16 he inherited a considerable fortune on the death of his father and in 1748 set out on a grand tour of the continent. In 1755, he set out on a further journey to Lisbon following the earthquake which struck the city in that year and was captured, en route, by French privateers. He spent a short time in French prisons, which awoke his interest in the question of imprisonment and on his return to England he settled into the life of a prosperous country gentleman, close to the home of his even more prosperous cousin, Samuel Whitbread, who had already made a considerable fortune from brewing.

In 1773 he was appointed High Sheriff of Bedfordshire, a position in which little was expected of him, but he decided to take the role seriously and inspect the county prison. He was shocked by what he saw and in particular by the discovery that many prisoners were held despite being innocent because they could not pay the gaoler's release fee. Having given evidence on this and other related matters to a Parliamentary Committee in 1774, he then embarked upon a tour of the prisons of England, Scotland and Wales, which resulted in a report called 'The State of the Prisons' in 1777. By 1784, Howard estimated that he had travelled over 40,000 miles on his inspection visits. He always travelled on horseback because, he explained, if he were to travel in the greater comfort of a carriage, he would carry with him the intolerable smell of the gaols he had visited. In 1789, he undertook a final journey to visit prisons in Eastern Europe, the Ukraine and Russia. He contracted typhus ('prison fever) and was buried on the shores of the Black Sea near Odessa in the Ukraine.

Howard's reports spurred the government, at the very time that prison sentences were becoming a form of punishment in themselves, to introduce a number of reforms which were long overdue. The practice of selling the office of 'keeper' to the highest bidder and encouraging the successful bidders to reclaim the fees from the unfortunate inmates was gradually phased out, as was the gaoler's release fee by an Act passed in 1774. Howard also made recommendations on the design of prisons and the regimes which should apply in them, which influenced Jeremy Bentham and others. The Howard League for Penal Reform, founded in 1866, continues the work that he began. John Howard was the first civilian to be commemorated by a statue in St Paul's Cathedral and the extent of his international influence is marked by statues as far away as the Ukraine as well as those set into the gatehouses of Wormwood Scrubs and Shrewsbury prisons.

THE QUAKER: 'POOR LITTLE INFANTS WITHOUT CLOTHING'

Elizabeth Fry (1780–1845) was born in Norwich into a prosperous Quaker family as Elizabeth Gurney and was related to the founders of Barclays Bank. She married into another Quaker banking family when she became the wife of Joseph Fry in 1800. By this time she had come under the influence of an American Quaker called William Savery and began to visit the poor of Norwich and its prisoners. Early Quakers had experience of the prison system as its inmates, since the founder of the movement George Fox (1624–91) and William Penn (1644–1718), had both been imprisoned in the previous centuries. A family friend called Stephen Grellet had visited Newgate Prison in 1813 and had been shocked by the conditions in which the inmates lived. Prompted by Grellet, Elizabeth visited the gaol in February of that year, recording her feelings in letters to her children:

> I have lately been twice to Newgate to see after the poor prisoners who had poor little infants without clothing, or with very little, and I think if you saw how small a piece of bread they are allowed each day you would be very sorry.

She wrote to her brother-in-law Thomas Buxton, another Quaker banker, in more severe terms of 'the filth, the closeness of the rooms, the furious manner and expressions of the women towards each other and the abandoned wickedness'. Buxton was a Member of Parliament and campaigned on Elizabeth's behalf. Elizabeth was particularly moved by the condition of a young woman who had killed her baby and faced death. She could do nothing for the young mother, who was presumably suffering post-natal depression but, with the assistance of a group of Quaker women, she set up a school for the children who were imprisoned with their parents and classes in needlework for the women. The women reacted very positively to the first kindness that many of them had ever known and, with the assistance of the keeper, who had regarded his charges as beyond hope, a matron was appointed to oversee their health.

Elizabeth approached Richard Dixon and company, based in Fenchurch Street, who supplied the convict settlements in Australia's Botany Bay and who agreed to buy the garments that the Newgate women made. The profits were invested in improvements in the women's diets and living conditions. John Randolph, the American ambassador, recorded, 'I have seen Elizabeth Fry in Newgate and I have witnessed there miraculous effects of true Christianity upon the most depraved of human beings'. Lord Byron was more cynical. While praising her work, he suggested that it would be better directed against the real sinners who inhabited the dissolute court of George IV at Carlton House:

> Oh Mrs Fry! Why go to Newgate? Why
> Preach to poor rogues; and wherefore not begin with
> Carlton or with other houses? Try
> Your hand at hardened and imperial sin.

STOP THE WHIPPING OF WOMEN

Elizabeth was now well known and began to campaign for better conditions for female prisoners in other gaols and, in particular, for female prisoners to be supervised by female officers. In 1817 she persuaded the government to cease the practice of whipping women prisoners. She also argued for more humane regimes in lunatic asylums and workhouses, and created London's first night shelter for the homeless after seeing the body of a young boy in the winter of 1819–20. She also founded a nurse training school at Guy's Hospital, an achievement later acknowledged by Florence Nightingale when she founded the Nightingale School at St Thomas's many years later, and took some of Elizabeth's trained nurses to Scutari.

Elizabeth also gave evidence to parliamentary committees as John Howard had done, met Queen Victoria and Prince Albert and was a guest at the Lord Mayor's banquet, an almost unprecedented honour for a woman. Many of the reforms sought by John Howard and Elizabeth were finally achieved in Robert Peel's Gaols Act of 1823, which specified that gaolers should receive a salary and that prisons should be inspected by magistrates. She also ensured that prisoners taken from prisons to the hulks were conveyed in covered carriages to spare them the jeers of the crowd as they travelled. The remission of up to a third of sentences for prisoners who showed signs of mending their ways followed her death in Ramsgate in 1845. As a memorial to her, a committee led by the Lord Mayor established a refuge for the destitute in Hackney. It later became a probation hostel for women and moved to Reading in 1958.

THE FIRST BORSTAL

John Howard and Elizabeth Fry had introduced a note of humanity to the harsh utilitarianism of Bentham, and other reforms followed. Later in the century, separate prisons were introduced for young offenders, beginning in the village of Borstal in Kent, though in the twenty-first century, prisons remain places where inmates are more likely to learn bad habits from one another than they are to learn skills to carry into a fresh start in life when they are released. Many of her ideas remain aspirations rather than achievements.

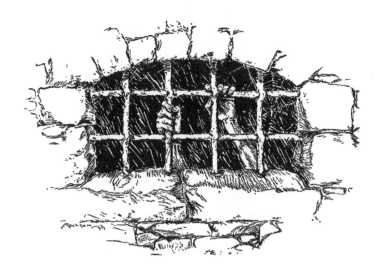